D1879841

THE INDO-ARYANS,

THEIR HISTORY, CREED AND PRACTICE

Owing to the antiquity and rarity of this book, certain pages are regrettably absent, and readability is compromised due to the blurring of the original text. If you possess any insights regarding the availability of these missing sections, kindly inform us. Your assistance is crucial in ensuring the completion of this significant work for the benefit of future generations.

THE INDO-ARYANS,

THEIR HISTORY, CREED AND PRACTICE

BY

RAMACHANDRA GHOSHA

GYAN

Published by

Gyan Publishing House
5, Ansari Road
Daryaganj, New Delhi-110002
Phone: 011-47034999, 9811692060
E-mail: books@gyanbooks.com

Distribution Network
gyanbooks.com
India, USA, Canada, UK, Australia

© Publisher

All rights reserved. No part of this work may be reproduced, stored, adapted, or transmitted in any form or by any means, electronic, mechanical, photocopying, micro-filming, recording or otherwise, or translated in any language, without the prior written permission of the copyright owner and the publisher.

ISBN: 978-93-6280-354-2 (HB)
First Published, 1881

2nd Impression 2024

Printed at: Gyan Press, Delhi.

The book is sold subject to the condition that it shall not, by way of trade or otherwise, be lent, resold, hired out, or otherwise circulated without the prior publisher's written consent.

THE INDO-ARYANS, THEIR HISTORY, CREED AND PRACTICE
Author: RAMACHANDRA GHOSHA

THE INDO-ARYANS,

THEIR HISTORY, CREED AND PRACTICE.

BY

RAMACHANDRA GHOSHA, F.R.S.L.,

MEMBER OF THE ROYAL ASIATIC SOCIETY, LONDON.

CALCUTTA:

B. BANERJEE & CO., 25-27, CORNWALLIS STREET.

1881.

TO

THE REV. K. M. BANERJEA, LL. D.,

HON. M. R. A. S., F. U. C.,

HONORARY CHAPLAIN TO THE BISHOP OF CALCUTTA.,

WHO OCCUPIES A CONSPICUOUS POSITION AMONG THE EMINENT SCHOLARS OF THE DAY, AND WHO HAS PLACED THE STUDENT OF VAIDIK LITERATURE UNDER DEEP AND LASTING OBLIGATION BY HIS RECENT SUCCESSFUL ATTEMPT TO ESTABLISH THE RELATION BETWEEN THE RIG-VEDA AND THE ASSYRIAN INSCRIPTIONS,

THIS VOLUME

IS DEDICATED AS A SINCERE MARK OF PROFOUND REGARD AND DEEP GRATITUDE,

BY HIS AFFECTIONATE FRIEND,

THE AUTHOR.

PREFACE.

THE precise object of the following pages is to present to the reader certain facts regarding the history, creed and practice of the Indo-Aryans, as far as these can be obtained from a study of ancient Sanskrit Literature. In taking up such extensive and complicated subjects I had to work up the materials which I had collected for many years; and these materials often so much embarrassed me by their copiousness and diversity that I had little hope of benefiting from them. There is, indeed, a dense mist of prejudice and preconceived opinions which always impede such investigations. But it should be frankly stated that great advances have since been made in the field of Sanskrit research, though much remains as uncertain and unsettled as before. The laborers in the field have now greatly increased; and their researches reflect lasting honor upon them. I need not give their names here when I have referred to them so frequently in the text and in the foot-notes; but I should only acknowledge with deep gratitude that I have greatly availed myself of their writings.

The Vedas are the gigantic labors of the Hindû mind. They have already attracted the attention of some of the best scholars of Europe and America. They are guidebooks in all researches into the civilization of the ancient Hindûs, on which history cannot throw the least light; though it must be admitted that the information to be gleaned from them is very scanty. Indeed, India never produced a Xenophon or a Thucydides;

but nevertheless history can be built up from the materials which lie buried in those ancient documents, by simply distinguishing facts from the shoals of mystical legends and mythological drapery which are found to envelop them. The age in which the Vedas and their appendages were composed, has exercised the blandest influence upon all succeeding periods of Indian history; every later branch of literature is closely connected with the Vaidik traditions; the religious and moral ideas have been derived from them; the later mythology has also developed out of them; and the Hindû life, in all its aspects, has been moulded by old traditionary precepts.

Though the researches of occidental *savans* into the Vedas are alike profound and accurate, they carry us into a labyrinth of heterogeneous materials, which to digest and at last to present in a readable shape is indeed a hard task. The general deductions and opinions of one Sanskritist in the West are in some cases not found to tally with those of his brother Sanskritist. Thus in many cases they, far from helping us to attain the truth, often throw great doubts and confusion on many an important and salient point. I have, therefore, generally avoided raising issues with them whenever I happened to find myself to differ widely from any one of them on such controverted points, and have only tried to arrive at a definite conclusion whenever that was possible. To claim to have certainly arrived at a literary truth is highly presumptuous in a country such as we live in, where the spirit of Niebuhr has not as yet been attained.

At all events their contributions towards ancient Sanskrit Literature have elucidated many knotty problems; which could never have been solved by the Indian Pandits, who hardly possess a scientific turn of mind; and have at last brought to our knowledge an immense store of information of vital importance which had been so long hid from us by the dishonorable attempts of the Brahmans, who debarred all but themselves from reading the Vedas. It is, however, a curious commentary on the vicissitudes of human affairs that the proud descendants of the holy *Ri*shis should consume their midnight oil on the banks of the Ganges, over their sacred books, published for the first time on the banks of the Neckar and the Thames, by those, whom they look upon as Mlechhas.

My warmest thanks are due to my esteemed friend the Hon'ble Pyârîmohana Mukhopâdhyâya, of Uttarapara, for kindly placing at my disposal various books and manuscripts a reference to which was necessary in preparing these pages for publication.

R. G.

CALCUTTA, *May*, 1881.

CONTENTS.

THE INDO-ARYANS.

CHAPTER I.

The Earliest History of the Indo-Aryan Family.

CENTRAL ASIA was probably the earliest point of ethnic movement, the homestead of the human family, the common abode of those races which have hitherto guided the van of civilization. The languages and mythologies of almost all the great historic races, however now widely separated, beckon to that country as their common dwelling place. Amidst the recesses of that focus of radiation and cradle of historic races, lie the materials of forty centuries of human history. When such dubious half-blind guides as mythology and tradition fail to penetrate into what lie in the pre-historic deeps, the languages can only with scientific certainty point out the way. So comparative Philology has been very appropriately called linguistic Palæontology. A study of the morphology and grammar of the Sanskrit in its oldest form, and of the Celtic, Greek, Latin, Lettish, Slavonic and Persian, shows us that all these languages sprung out of the same parent tongue, now extinct. It follows, therefore, as a necessary corollary that the nations, which spoke these languages, were also descended from one and the same stock; and they once constituted one united people.* Affinity in language certainly affords some presumption of affinity in race; but it is not in languages alone that an affinity exists between the Indians, the Iranians, the Greeks, and the Romans; their mythologies also imply a community of origin, and no doubt they yield some data for ethnic deductions. At any rate, the cradle of the Indo-Aryans is to be sought for in some country external to India; and the facts which have been brought to light enable us to determine the region in which the whole Aryan family must have lived together.

The Aryans, in the childhood of their history, were savages; and lived upon the flesh of wild animals which they hunted. They had not even huts to live in; but generally formed a small gang either for protecting themselves from dangers to which they were naturally exposed; or for hunting wild beasts for the purposes of food. They gradually passed to pastoral life; pastures now formed their territory and cattle their wealth. They soon acquired quiet and harmless habits, and became sober and diligent. They also became encircled by large families. In this manner, a number of clans were formed; and the gotra system is founded on a division into such clans. The shepherd easily became the leader of his clan; while the hunter, as a mere adventurer, could not take the lead, because his influence over his gang was by no means permanent. They now carried on agriculture and developed it; and also appreciated permanent property in the land. They con-

* Weber's Indische Skizzen, p. 7.

structed permanent habitations; and their diet was much improved. Chivalry is, in fact, the outgrowth of a desire of luxury; and the necessity of self-defence promotes the growth of feudalism. After thus passing through many vicissitudes of fortune they gradually formed themselves into a feudal community governed by the same religious and social institutions, and the same political organisation. Small states were thus formed; and there is no doubt that the Indo-Aryans reached this stage of civilization before they immigrated into India. But when they advanced from one stage of civilization to another they did by no means give up all their former institutions and customs; nor did they discard the religious and social polity, to which they had once become attached.

The pre-emigration events as recorded in the *Ṛig*-veda, which again are confirmed by the Zand-Avesta and the Assyrian Inscriptions, and by a legend in the *Ṡata*patha-Brâhma*n*a (i. 2, 5, 1 ff), naturally point to the west of Asia for the primitive home of the Aryans; and also to the migratory route of the Indo-Aryans and the Persa-Aryans from "the West to the East." Our ancestors as well speak of their "old home," the *pratna okas*;* but cannot give its geography. In the *Ṛig*-veda an expression also occurs which might lead us to suppose that the Indo-Aryans still retained some reminiscences of their having at one time occupied a colder country.† And in the allusions made to the northerly region of the Uttarakurus there may be some recollections of their early connexion

* *Ṛig*-veda, i. 30, 9.

† *Ṛig*-veda, i 64, 14; v. 54, 15; vi. 10, 7; vi. 12, 6; vi. 13. 6; vi. 17, 15.

with the countries to the north of the Himâlayas.* Ptolemy (Geogr. vi. 16) was also acquainted with the Uttarakurus. According to Lassen the Ottorokora (οττοροκόρα) of Ptolemy must be sought for to the east of Kashghar. There is again a tradition in the First Fargard of the Vendîdâd regarding the earliest abodes of the Aryan race. The description contained in it is simply of the gradual diffusion or rather of the first sixteen settlements of the Aryan race. The Airyana-vaêjô is first spoken of in it; but its locality is not mentioned, nor is its geography given. It means the Aryan residence; and by it we are to understand the original country of the Aryans. We have here undoubtedly geographical descriptions of some real countries. Of the sixteen lands alluded to nine did certainly exist; and we know their geographical positions. The Airyana-vaêjô could be localised in the basin of the Araxes which was identified with the Oxus in the time of Herodotus. However, the admission of the *pratna okas* on the part of our ancestors shows clearly that they came to India from beyond the Indus; and moreover the testimonies which have been brought to light point to Media as that home, the *officina gentium* whence issued swarms of men whose descendants now constitute the most civilized nations of the earth; and the migration of those men apparently belongs to a period far beyond the reach of documentary history. Afterwards a Turanian invasion of Media was probably the cause of the gradual dispersion of the whole family on all sides. They must have travelled away from their primeval abodes, at different times, and in different direc-

* Aitareya-Brâhmana, viii. 14. Weber's Indische Studien, i. p. 218.

tions. It is not, however, easy to define their routes ; some of course went westward, others eastward.* Those that went westward were the first to break off from their pristine home ; and those that came eastward were the last of the emigrants. Probably after many defections in the course of their migration some of them may have remained behind, and established themselves in different countries. But those that came eastward had to encounter on their way the conflicts which are recorded in the Veda and the Zand-Avesta ; and this also receives confirmation from the temporary disappearance of Vishnu from them in their marches. Their marches were, no doubt, something like religious processions regularly worshipping and performing their ceremonial acts, the rear and flank guards repeating hymns in the Vaidik seven metres,† and the vanguard bearing the holy fire in the front.‡

After crossing the narrow passes of the Hindukush, the eastern branch first settled on the north-western frontiers of India, in the Panjâb, and even beyond the Panjâb on the Kubhâ.§ In the Panjâb they continued to form one community for a considerable time ;‖ and they lived on equal terms so far as the worship of the Sun and Fire and the elements of Nature was concerned. They had also the primitive institution of sacrifices ; though they differed among themselves as to their scope and the mode

* Banerjea's Arian Witness, p. 111.

† *Rig*-veda, i. 22, 16.

‡ Muir's Sanskrit Texts, iv. 122.

§ Weber's Indische Studien, iv. p. 379, n.

‖ Müller's Last Results of the Persian Researches, p. 113 ; and his Lectures on the Science of Language, i. p. 235.

of conducting them. But one party insisted on the actual completion of the sacrifice as the *Vashat*; while the other would not allow it. Nor would the latter sanction even the use of the Soma drink by which the former set store.* There were also some principal doctrinal differences between both the parties; and such religious differences only separated the one from the other.† There are certainly historical allusions to the schism both in the Veda and in the Avesta. But according to Haug the causes of the schism were not only of a religious but also of a social and political nature.‡ And both the parties latterly formed again two other branches, the Indo-Aryans and the Persa-Aryans. Now each branch bore feelings of bitterness against the other; and many were the sanguinary conflicts which took place between them. It also appears from the *R*ig-veda that Ish*t*âsva or the Sanskrit transliteration of Vîshtâspa of the Zand-Avesta, who was the patron of Zoroaster§ and the promoter of his doctrines, had contemplated the forcible imposition of his prophet's teaching on all around him by fire and sword.‖ But the ancestors of the Indo-Aryans refused manfully to submit to such religious intolerance; and they strenuously defended their own religion. "What can Ish*t*âsva," said they, "what can Ish*t*arasmi, rulers of the world as they are, do against our

* Yasna, xxxii. 3; xlviii. 10; see also Haug's Essays, p. 291.

† Bleeck, Introduction to the Avesta, p. x.; Müller's Last Results of the Persian Researches, p. 112; and his Chips from a German Workshop, i. p. 83.

‡ Haug's Essays, p. 292.

§ In the *R*ig-veda (vii. 37, 7) this name appears in the corrupt form of Jaradashti.

‖ Farvardan-yast, xiii. 99.

protecting men?"* As to who this Vîshtâspa was we are still in the dark, but he must have been different from the father of Darius, as he was a more ancient character.

Bhrigu originated pyro-cultus (*R*ig-veda, i. 58, 6; i. 60, 1; x. 122, 5), and promoted the celebration of sacrificial ceremonies in the world at large; and there can be no doubt that our ancestors, who composed the eastern branch of the Aryan race, were originally Fire-worshippers (i. 1, 2). They also no doubt recognised two principles, one the supreme principle of Good and the other the principle of Evil. In the Zand-Avesta the supreme principle of Good is called Ahura Mazda, which means the *all-knowing or wise Lord.* This name precisely corresponds with Asura-pracheta (iv. 53, 1) in the *R*ig-veda. And Angrô-mainyush, the spirit of Evil or Sin in the Zand-Avesta, is also identical with Nir*r*iti (i. 24, 9) of the Veda. But here it should be candidly stated that, according to the Zand-Avesta, Ahura Mazda and Angrô-mainyush are independent creators of good and evil respectively; while, according to the Veda, Nir*r*ti is not "an uncreate eternal substance."† In the Assyrian empire Asur was an appellative for God; and the eastern branch may have accepted the term from the Assyrians. In the older portions of the *R*ig-veda the appellative is used in as good a sense as in the Zand-Avesta; and so we find the Maruts (i. 64, 2), Indra (i. 54, 3), Varu*n*a (ii. 27, 10), Tvash*t*ri (i. 110, 3), Agni (v. 12–1), Vâyu (v. 42, 1), Pûshan (v. 51, 11), Savit*r*i (v. 49, 2), Parjanya (v. 63. 3, 7), and other gods termed or accosted

* *R*ig-veda, i. 122, 13.

† Banerjea's Essays, p. 53.

as Asuras. But in these portions again the epithet is used, though only twice, in a bad sense (ii. 32, 4 ; vii. 99, 5) i. e. evil spirits or obstructors of religious rites and ceremonies. The term Asura was also applicable both to the Assyrian nation and to the follower of Ahura Mazda. Again, the Indo-Aryans were called Daêvas in the Zand-Avesta, and the Zoroastrians were in like manner called Asuras in the Veda. The term Asura, in its bad sense, was either intended for the Assyrians as a nation or for the intolerant Zoroastrians. And thus the contradictory senses of the name can only be accounted for by the fact that either because there arose the *odium theologicum* between the Indo-Aryans and the Persa-Aryans, or because the Indo-Aryans had national antipathy for they had the bitter recollections of the barbarous atrocities which the Assyrian kings boastingly practised against them when they once lived under the yoke of Assyria (Asur).

They must have penetrated into India not all at once, but in successive waves of immigration. The Indo-Aryans, after the Persa-Aryans had separated from them, and migrated westward to Arachosia and Persia, (in this period the Aryan mind blended with the Semitic, and no doubt it was the most momentous period in their history which surely opened another stage of religious thought) gradually spread towards the east, beyond the Sarasvatî, and over Hindustan as far as the Ganges ;* and afterwards diffused themselves to the south of the peninsula. Many centuries were of course required to subjugate the wild and vigorous aborigines, to break down their residences, and to

* Weber's Indische Studien, ii. p. 20.

bring them over to Brahmanism. The Indo-Aryans so isolated themselves from their primitive settlement as to have lost in a very short time all sympathy for their cousins. And after they had got a home in India, they began to ignore all trans-Indus events, and to declare themselves as the autochthones of Indian soil.* In India they must have established themselves by household groups, each occupying a specifically assigned area within the boundaries of which the intruders were only allowed to settle upon terms of subjection. Though bound together by the feelings of a common descent, language and religion, and by their joint hostility to the aborigines, they were divided into clans quite separate from one another. They were now communities of free men. In such a state the position of an individual member was as the head of a family and the master of wealth.† Now they stood in constant alarm of the aborigines; and they were often engaged in hostilities with them, and even with the members of their own community, simply with a view to be enriched with the booty.‡ The country they now occupied was partly cultivated, and partly covered by forests. And it was no doubt peopled by various tribes,§ and divided into numerous principalities.||

At such primitive times when they were all a pastoral and agricultural people, there could exist no distinct caste

* Banerjea's Arian Witness, pp. 30, 41.

† Whitney's Oriental and Linguistic Studies, p. 25.

‡ *Ṛig*-veda, i. 73, 5.

§ Roth's Literature and History of the Veda, pp. 131, ff.

|| Wilson's *Ṛig*-veda, i. p. xliii.

of cultivators of the earth ; when they were all warriors there could be no military caste ; and when each member of the community had the privilege to approach the gods with his own prayers and offerings there could be no sacerdotal order. Then the castes had no existence. At the time when the Indo-Aryans left their original home, and set foot on Indian soil, they naturally came into contact with the Dasyus or the aborigines of India. These people, forming the Turanian branch of the human family, differed widely from the Indo-Aryans, in their physical appearance and color, language and manners. Under such divergence, there was no ground for the establishment or conservation of feelings of amity and unity between the classes. Consequently, the Indo-Aryans and the Dasyus frequently found themselves in the bitterest conflict. The Indo-Aryans, as they were naturally of fair complexion, of majestic appearance, civilized and much more advanced in thought, looked down upon the aborigines who were of beastly appearance. In the Veda, the aborigines are frequently called Dasyus or Dâsas ;* and the Indo-Aryans, with a certain degree of hatred, called them *tvacham krishnâm*† or the "blackskin." From the Veda, we obtain sufficient evidence of there having been a wide difference and natural enmity between them ; and the Indo-Aryans are found scornfully to apply to the Dasyus the terms of *avrata* (vi. 14, 3.), *apavrata* (v. 42, 9.), *ayajyu* (i. 131, 4.) *abrahma* (iv. 16, 9.), *anindra* (i. 133, 1.), etc. The

* *Rig-veda*, i. 103, 3 ; i. 117, 21 ; vi. 25, 2, 3; vi. 60, 6 ; vii. 83, 1 ; x. 38, 3 ; x. 86, 19 ; x. 102, 3 ; x. 83, 1.

† *Rig-veda*, i. 130, 8 ; ix.41, 1.

main difference consisted in color and feature ; and hence *varna* gradually came to imply caste. Caste then was purely an ethnological institution. In the Veda varna appears in the sense of color (i. 73, 7 ; i. 113, 2), of bright color or light (iii. 34, 5), and of race, the white and the dark (ii. 12, 4 ; iii. 34, 8, 9).

In several places of the *R*ig-veda, five classes are generally spoken of such as *pancha-krishtayah*, *pancha-kshitayah*, *pancha-charshanayah*, *pancha-janâh*, *pancha-bhûma*, and *pancha-jâtâ*. There is no clue to be found for the better understanding of what tribal divisions or social classifications these classes implied. Mankind, in a collective sense, are said to be distinguished into five classes. Sâyana, following the received tradition of his own time, explains these terms as denoting the four castes with the Nishâdas or the aborigines for a fifth. Yâska, in Nirukta (iii. 8), referring to the opinions of older schools, says that these five classes of beings are the *Gandharvas*, *Pitris*, *Devas*, *Asuras*, and *Rakshases*, and according to some the four castes, and the aborigines or Nishâdas. But these meanings seem quite immaterial, and are merely imaginary. When the five classes are designated by so many distinct appellatives, and especially by such a one as *pancha-bhûma*, it appears that these classifications arose possibly from the different localities the Indo-Aryans first occupied after their advent to India. The authors of the hymns of the *R*ig-veda regarded Manu as the common progenitor of the whole of the Aryan people, either the priests or the chiefs, or those that formed the mass of the population.* This

* *R*ig-veda, i. 80, 16 ; i. 114, 2 ; ii. 33, 13 ; viii. 52, 1 ; viii. 30, 3.

notion of descent from one common father overthrows altogether the supposition that the Aryan nation originally consisted of four different castes.

From the mass of the population were formed in course of time two privileged classes, a priesthood and an aristocracy. But after the population had greatly increased a division of labor soon became a necessity. The more contemplative among them betook themselves to the worship of the gods, and to the performance of rites and ceremonies at the holy altars ; the more powerful class held rule over the rest ; and the majority of the population followed various occupations ; while the aborigines incorporated themselves in the Indo-Aryan community either as slaves* or as handicraftsmen. The priesthood was formed only from the employment by the chiefs of individuals known for their rhythmical faculty, knowledge of sacred things, and sanctity, to officiate at the worship of the gods ; and the aristocracy was formed properly from the class of petty kings. The families of those kings who held sway over single tribes came gradually to occupy a more and more prominent position in the larger kingdoms which were of necessity founded ; and thus the military caste was formed. And the people proper, the visas, formed a third caste. The term Vaisya does not occur in any other hymns of the *R*ig-veda, but in the Purusha-sûkta ; and only once in the Atharvan (v. 17, 9). The Vaisyas formed the mass of the people ; the word being derived from vis which means the general community. But the *S*ûdras were a mixed body, partly composed of the aborigines themselves, partly

* *R*ig-veda, viii. 46, 32 ; Vâlkhilya 8, 3.

of those Aryans who had settled earlier in India, and partly of those recruits from the later Aryan emigrants who threw off the Brahmanical yoke.* But the condition of the *Sûdras* was not so wretched then as it was afterwards. They were allowed to attend the ceremonies; and they even took an active part on such occasions. The *Ṛig* and the Atharva vedas throw an immense blaze of light on the relations of the different classes of Indian society to one another at the time when they were formed. From the later hymns of the *Ṛig*-veda we learn that the priesthood had already become a profession; but there are other indications also which justify the conclusion that there was no discrimination of profession; and even there are numerous references to be found in all parts of the hymn-collection to a variety of ranks, classes and professions however without any rigid prescriptions about them. The three highest castes stood in a more intimate relation with one another either in point of descent or culture, than any of them did to the fourth.

We have, however, no knowledge of the political condition of the Indo-Aryans, beyond the specification of the names of some princes. These names are peculiar to the Veda. We have particular mention, not only of kings, but of envoys (ii. 127, 9) and heralds (ii. 127, 10). The kings sent ambassadors to one another (i. 71, 4); and also employed spies. The political institutions of those days very closely resembled those of the Homeric Greeks. The names for king meant father of the house, and headman of the tribe. Each state was governed by

* Roth's Literature and History of the Veda, p. 117; Weber's History of Indian Literature, p. 18.

a king, whose office was often hereditary; but also sometimes elective. Kings are mentioned in the hymns;* and rulers or governors under the titles of pûrapati† and grâmanî‡ are also alluded to. These rulers held powers subject to certain obligations towards a king. The existence of the office of kings, and the imposition of taxes (i. 70, 5), or contributions from the people for the maintenance of kingdoms certainly imply a settled state of government. The government was good;§ and even the village system existed during that period. Meetings of princes are alluded to (x. 97, 6). The princes were always surrounded by faithful friends (i. 73, 3); and they always took delight in listening to the bards (i. 27, 12). There were also halls of justice (ii. 124, 7); and the complicated law of inheritance (iii. 31, 1–2) was to a certain extent in force; and our ancestors had conceptions of the rights of property and definite guarantees for their preservation, had formalities for transactions of exchange and sale (iii. 24, 9), for payment of wages, and for the administration of oath. (A. V. iv. 16). The laws of contract were developed. Debts and debtors are even adverted to (ii. 24, 13; ii. 28, 9); and sometimes exorbitant interest was charged (iii. 53, 14). The tricks of trade were also known in those days.

Their chief possessions were the flocks and herds; but they by no means neglected the cultivation of the earth.

* *Rig-veda*, i. 40, 8; i. 126, 1; iii. 43, 5; v. 37, 4; x. 33, 4.

† Ibid, i. 173, 10.

‡ Ibid, x. 62, 11.

§ Ibid, i. 173.

Cultivated and fertile lands (iii. 41, 6 ; iv. 20, 1) and water-courses are alluded to ;* and the irrigation of lands under cultivation is also recommended (ii. 122, 6). They sunk wells (i. 30, 1), and dug channels (ii. 28, 5). They measured their fields with rods (i. 110, 5). Oxen ploughed their fields (vi. 20, 19); and the articles of food were brought home in waggons and carts. We read of a husbandman repeatedly ploughing the earth for barley (i. 23, 15). They had also granaries (ii. 14, 11).

They had pasturage (i. 67, 3); and domesticated the cow, the sheep, the goat, the horse, and the dog. And the zoology of the *Rig*-veda comprises a great many other animals, such as lions, tigers, bears, wolves, elephants, oxes, camels, deers, antelopes, hogs, asses, rams, bulls, serpents, mosquitoes, bees, mares, scorpions, worms, snakes, fishes, crocodiles, porpoises, apes, owls, boars, buffaloes, jackals, mices, foxes, frogs, rats, and different kinds of birds, *i. e.* peacocks, eagles, pigeons, vultures, ducks, swans, kites, crows, quails, falcons, etc.

The community consisted of the rich and the poor.† The rich were no doubt over-bearing (i. 145, 2) ; and the middle classes pursued their trades and lived in comfort. But the lower classes lived from hand to mouth (iv. 25, 8). Labor was valued (i. 79, 1) ; and the spirit of adventure and enterprise was also appreciated (i. 17, 31). The different occupations pursued were those of priests, poets, physicians, barbers, wood-cutters, carpenters, black-smiths, female grinders of corn, carriage builders, workers in wood and metal, manufacturers of weapons of war and other sharp-

* *Rig*-veda, iii. 45, 3 ; x. 43, 7.

† Ibid, x. 117.

edged implements, boat and ship builders, rope makers, and butchers. The bhisty with his skin brought them water; and the groom rubbed down their horses (ii. 135, 5).

They thought of the means of transit from the earliest times. They had good and great roads (i. 116, 20), suitable and little paths (i. 58, 1; iv. 16, 3) easy to be traversed in mountainous regions and inaccessible places. At the resting-places on the road refreshments were always kept ready (ii. 166, 9). They navigated in oared boats (ii. 131, 2) and ferries.* They were a maritime and mercantile nation; sea-going ships and navigation in the open sea were familiar to them. They were not content with internal trade; they also undertook sea-voyages as we read of merchants sailing for gain.† Metal money had been in use; *nishkas* of gold being mentioned.‡ The use of money in trade may not have been unknown, for "merchants desirous of gain" are cited in the *R*ik, as sending their ships to the sea.§ We also read of *suvarnas*; and a *suvarna*, according to Colebrooke, was equal to sixteen mâshâs. They were not only familiar with the oceans; but sometimes must have engaged in naval expeditions.‖ And there is mention made of a naval expedition under Bhujyu, the son of Tugra, against a foreign island, which was frustrated only by shipwreck. (i. 116, 3—5).

* *R*ig-veda, ii. 37.

† Ibid, i. 307.

‡ Ibid, i. 126. According to Manu (vii. 134) a *nishka* was a weight of gold equal to four *suvarnas*. Yâska, in his Nirukta, p. 13, quotes from the Veda, eighteen different words, which convey the abstract idea of wealth, without having any reference to grain, or cattle, or any other object.

§ *R*ig-veda, i. 48, 3; i. 56, 2.

‖ Ibid, i. 116, 3.

There were cities (pur) as distinct from villages (grâma).* We read of "cities of stone," of "cities made of iron,"† and of cities with a hundred surrounding walls,‡ which convey the idea of forts consisting of a series of concentric walls. When we read of iron cities we should take them as more substantial than wattle and mud.

They lived in permanent habitations ; and their houses were roofed, and had windows and doors (i.113,4). Generally their houses were guarded by dogs. Bricks (ishtakâ) were made and known ; and lime, mortar, and stucco were used for the purpose of plastering them (iv. 47, 2). The words which occur in the Veda signifying a house attest to the existence of brick and stone buildings. We read of a "house having a thousand doors,"§ of "a palace supported by a thousand columns,"‖ of "stately mansion" (i. 101, 8), of "lowly dwelling" (i. 101, 8), of a "destitute dwelling" (i. 104, 7), of the "spacious dwelling-place" (i. 36, 8), of "stone houses," of "carved stones," and of "brick edifices." There were also halls "vast, comprehensive and thousand-doored." Vasishtha longs for a "three storied dwelling" (v. 101, 2) ; and Atri is said to have been "thrown into a machine room with a hundred doors where he was roasted" (i. 51, 3).

They lived together with their sons and grandsons ; and their domestic economy was founded upon the principles

* *Rig*-veda, i. 114. 1 ; i. 44, 10 ; i. 49, 4 ; x. 146, 1.

† Ibid, i. 58, 8; ii. 20, 8 ; iv. 27, 1; vii. 3, 7 ; vii. 15, 14 ; vii. 95, 1; viii. 89, 8; x. 101, 8.

‡ Ibid, i. 166, 8 ; vii. 15, 14.

§ Ibid, vii. 88, 5.

‖ Ibid, ii. 41, 5.

of the joint-family system (i. 114, 6). They were never weary of relatives (ii. 29, 4). In other respects their conception of a home approached that of the English—"a pleasant abode,"—"a well-dressed wife,"—"an irreproachable and beloved wife," "who ornaments the chamber of sacrifice," and "adorns a dwelling," and a "draught of wine." Husband and wife were both rulers of the house ; and no doubt there subsisted concord in the family (A. V. iii. 30). This trait in their domestic character illustrates the happiness of their family life. Although they rejoiced more at the birth of sons (i. 105, 3), who were in all cases inheritors of ancestral wealth (i. 73, 9) ; yet they showed tender affections for daughters. They used to hold social meetings (A. V. vii. 12) ; and were also disposed to profit by the healthy influences of the company of men possessing cultivated minds (A. V. vii. 12). The unmarried daughters had a claim upon their father, brother, or other male relatives for subsistence (ii. 17, 7). And even daughters had claims to a share of the paternal property (ii. 124, 7). Women were active in their occupations ; and for them there was needle-work.* The social position of women was considerably higher than it is in modern times. They are spoken of kindly and pleasantly, as "an ornament in a dwelling" (i. 66, 3). They could converse with their husbands on equal terms, and go together and attend the sacrifices. They were also quite at liberty to walk and ride abroad (ii. 166, 5) ; and were, without any reserve, present at public feasts and games. Lovely maidens appeared in a procession ; and grown up un-

* *Ṛig-veda*, ii. 288.

married daughters remained without reproach in their fathers' houses. Our ancestors cultivated the laws of morality and civil polity to a great extent. Their social instinct was as old as the religious. The ties of blood were most scrupulously respected; and the extent to which matrimony among blood-relations could not be allowed was interdicted. They had a marriage ceremonial;* but it is exceedingly difficult to determine in what manner the nuptial ceremonies were performed; and what rules were observed at such ceremonies. They had also wedding apparel, for there is mention made of the bride's garment (x. 85, 3, 34). On the occasion of the nuptial ceremonies, a wish was expressed, as a rule, in the bride's favor that she may be a queen over her father-in-law, her mother-in-law, her husband's sister, and his brothers (x. 85, 46). The priests gave spiritual instructions to the grown up brides as they parted with their parents (x. 85, 15). The maidens decorated themselves with unguents to go to their bridegrooms (iii. 58, 9). Early marriage by no means formed a rule; and the women enjoyed a freedom of choice in the selection of their husbands.† Remarriage of widows was not prohibited;‡ and mention is even made of the marriage of a widow with her deceased husband's brother.§ It is to be stated, however, that there is no mention of Sûdras as a class with which Brahmans intermarried. Although intermarriages between these two castes were dis-

* *Rig*-veda, x. 109; see also Weber's Indische Studien, v. p. 177ff.

† Ibid, x. 27, 11, 12; see also Taittirîya-Brâhma*n*a, ii. 4, 2, 7.

‡ Atharva-veda, ix. 5, 27f; see also Taittirîya-A'ra*n*yaka, vi. 1, 14.

§ *Rig*-veda, x. 40, 2.

approved, yet we can hardly believe that they were ever prohibited.* Polygamy was to a certain extent tolerated ;† though monogamy was the rule.‡ There are also references made to conjugal infidelity.§ There were even traces of the vices of civilization; for we read in the Veda of common women (ii. 167, 4), of secret births (ii. 29, 1), of gambling and intoxication (v. 86, 6), and of thieves (i. 42, 3). Prof. Weber advances some astounding proofs of the little confidence entertained in ancient times by the Indo-Aryans in the chastity of their women.‖ Notwithstanding all this women were held by the authors of the Brâhma*n*as in high estimation; but still there are other places in which they are spoken of disparagingly.** Adultery was no uncommon occurence ;†† and it is stated that the wife of the person offering *praghâsa* to Varu*n*a, must have one or more paramours.‡‡

Rice, barley, millet, and other kinds of grain, milk (ii. 137, 1), honey (ii. 139, 3), herbs (i. 90, 6), curd (ii. 137, 2), ripe fruits, butter and cheese (ii. 134, 6) were their usual meal. In the *R*ig-veda distinct references are made to barley (yava);§§ and mention of rice (vrîhi), beans (mâsha), and tila is made in the Atharvan.‖‖ Parched corn, (dhân),(a) boiled

* Vâjasaneyi-Sa*m*hitâ, 23, 30.

† *R*ig-veda, i. 62, 11; i. 71, 1; i. 105, 8; vii. 26, 3.

‡ Ibid, i. 105, 2; i. 124, 7.

§ Ibid, i. 167, 4; ix. 67, 10ff; x. 34. 4; x. 40, 6.

‖ Nidâna-Sûtra, iii. 8 ; see also *S*atapatha-Brâhma*n*a, iii. 2, 1, 40.

** Taittirîya-Sa*m*hitâ, vi. 5, 8, 2.

†† Taittirîya-Sa*m*hitâ, v. 6, 8, 3.

‡‡ *S*atapatha-Brâhma*n*a, ii. 5, 2, 20.

§§ *R*ig-veda, i. 23, 15 ; i. 66, 3 ; i. 117, 21 etc.

‖‖ vi. 140, 2.

(a) Ibid, i. 16, 2 ; iii, 35, 3 ; iii. 52, 5 ; vi. 29, 4.

rice (odana), cakes (upûpa), and meal prepared with curd or butter are mentioned.* Barley cakes mixed with milk (v. 2, 3), boiled milk and boiled barley are alluded to (ii. 187, 9). We also read of vegetable cakes of fried meal (ii. 187, 10). Fruit (phala) is referred to.† Bulls, rams, and buffaloes formed a portion of their food.‡ They were also beef eaters.§ It is true, that there was a time when bovine meat was actually deemed a delightful food, a token of generous hospitality in honor of a respected guest or *goghna.*‖ The slaughter of a cow on the arrival of a distinguished guest was invariably practised in India. This custom was so widely prevalent that *goghna* or "cow-killer" came to pass as a term for such a guest. Even Pâ*n*ini has given the etymology of "cow-killer" in the sense of a guest (iii. 4, 73). But it appears that the cow and one of its products (gomûtra) came to be regarded as sacred in the days of Patanjali, whose date has been fixed in the middle of the 2nd century B. C. Bovine meat was also considered as an essential accompaniment in the journey from this to the future world; so much so that a cow was in all cases burnt with the dead.

Cooking is described ;** and in preparing flesh meat, part was boiled in a caldron, part was roasted on spits, and

* *R*ig-veda iii. 52, 7 ; vi. 57, 2 ; see also Atharva-veda, xi. 3, 32 & 49.

† Ibid, iii. 45, 4.

‡ Ibid, i. 164, 43 ; v. 29, 7 ; viii. 12, 8 ; viii. 66, 10 ; x. 27, 2,

§ Wilson's *R*ig-veda, i. p. 165 ; iii. pp. 163, 276, 416 & 453.

‖ Asiatic Researches, vii. p. 288.

** *R*ig-veda, ii, 117 ; Atharva-veda, vi, 123, 4.

part was made into balls. There were vessels to distribute the broth; dishes with covers, and skewers and knives (ii. 162, 13). The queens and wives assisted in cooking and preparing the every day meal and the banquet. There were different kinds of earthen cooking pots (kapâlas). We read of kalasa or jar; and of kilns or furnaces for the baking of such vessels. And frequent mention is made of "potters," and of "potters' wheel." The material which was used in the manufacture of domestic vessels was not only clay, but also wood and leather, and even metals. They had "golden cups," plates of gold, silver, bronze, and magnetic iron; earthen vessels (v. 104, 21), wooden vessels and cups (ii, 175, 3; iv. 44, 5), leather skins for water, leather bottles and vessels (iii. 45, 1-3).

Wine was in use.* Swillers of wine are mentioned.† Our ancestors were greatly addicted to the drinking of spirits; and indulged excessively both in *soma* and other strong drinks. Wines or spirits were publicly sold in shops for the general use of the community. In the *R*ig-veda a hymn occurs which shows beyond all doubt that wine was kept in leather bottles,‡ and sold without any reserve to all comers. The Taittirîya-Brâhma*n*a contains *mantras* which speak of the preparation of the liquor; but no information is available as to how the distillation was effected.

Our ancestors made considerable progress in their dress. But no information is available regarding its form and shape. It is possible that the mass of the popu-

* *R*ig-veda, i. 116, 7; vii. 86, 6; x. 107, 9.

† Ibid, viii. 21, 14.

‡ Ibid, ii. 191, 10.

lation wore scarfs or plaidlike articles.* The *Rig*-veda contains many texts which show that they were perfectly familiar with the art of weaving. We read of "a woman weaving a garment" (ii. 38, 4), of "female weavers," (ii. 3, 6), of the warp and the woof (vi. 9. 1), of "putting on becoming attire," of "a well-attired female," of "a well-dressed woman," (iv. 80, 6), of "elegant garments" (iii. 3, 2), and of also "elegant well-made garments (x. 107, 9; v. 29, 15), as fit for honorary presents. In the Yajus and the Sâman there are many allusions to clothing; and in the former even "gold cloth" or "brocade" is mentioned.† Furs, skins, cotton, and wool (iii. 5, 4) were the only materials of which clothing was made; and even various colors were used in dyeing textile fabrics. It appears that white clothes were especially prized (iii. 39, 2). Silk is nowhere mentioned in the Veda; but Pâ*n*ini mentions it.‡ Mention of the needle and sewing has been met with; and there can be no doubt that our ancestors were familiar with dresses made with the aid of scissors§ and needle (ii. 32, 4). They wore turbans; and turban or head-dress under the name of *ushnîsha* is mentioned in the Atharva-veda (xv. 2, 1.)‖ Female modesty required the covering of the body down to the ankles; and the breasts were never to be exposed. Women always wore a sheet and kanchuka

* Mitra's Antiquities of Orissa, i. p. 81.

† Taittirîya-Brâhma*n*a, iii. 675.

‡ कोशाड्ढञ् । iv. 3, 42.

§ *Rig*-veda, viii. 4, 16.

‖ Muir's Sanskrit Texts, v. 462

over their clothes; and moved about with shoes or pattens on.*

The Indo-Aryans, as a rule, never cultivated the beard; and even in those early times razor (v. 4, 16) and barber were in every day requisition.† Allusions to shaving are also made.‡ Boots, shoes and pattens were also in fashion in those days. The material of which these were made was bovine leather. Pâ*n*ini gives words for boots; and according to *S*â*m*vatya as cited by A'*s*valâyana (iv. 9, 24), the hide of the sacrificial cattle was even used as material for shoes, and for other household articles. They had umbrellas.§ The ladies had an inordinate fondness for ornaments and for decoration of the different parts of the body (i. 85, 1). They also decorated themselves with garlands (iii. 38, 6); and even sons embellished themselves with ornaments (i. 85, 3). We read of "golden ornaments" (i. 35, 4), of "golden collars," "bracelets" (iv. 53, 4), and "fingerrings," of "an adorable uniform necklace" (ii. 33, 10), of "golden earrings," golden neck-chains, anklets, and of "jewel necklace" (ii. 122, 14). There is mention made of pearls (x. 68, 11), and golden tiaras (iv. 54, 11). In the Brâhma*n*a of the Yajur-veda jewellery is said to be strung in gold.‖ Whether looking glasses formed part of the toilet is very doubtful. They had musical instruments of shells and reeds; and there is mention made

* Bühler's A'pastamba, p. 14.

† *R*ig-veda, i. 92, 4; x. 142, 4.

‡ *R*ig-veda, x. 142, 4.

§ Pâ*n*ini, vi. 4, 97.

‖ Taittirîya-Brâhma*n*a, iii, 665.

of a harp with a hundred strings (i. 85, 10), and of melodious lutes (ii. 34, 13). Dancers afforded them entertainment;* and for their amusement they had also puppets (iii. 32, 23) and stage exhibitions.†

They had carriages and war chariots (iv. 63, 5) drawn by horses; and bullock carts and waggons (i. 30, 15). The carriages were made of wood and mounted on brazen wheels; and had iron reins and pillars. These carriages had seats‡ and awnings;§ and they were "easy going" (i. 13, 4), and sometimes "inlaid with gold." There were chariots, spacious and richly ornamented with three metals, gold, silver and copper; and fitted with golden trappings. We also read of "three columned triangular car" (i. 47, 2), of "golden three shafted chariots," of "golden wheels covered with iron weapons," and of "arming the wheels." In the *Ṛig*-veda "three benches as fixtures in each car and the space sufficient for several persons and some goods" are repeatedly mentioned (ii. 183, 1). They had also *kaśâ* or whips (i. 22, 3).

Gold, silver, copper and iron were known and worked. And they appear to have been the first to discover how to turn iron into steel. They used golden mail, raiment and helmet,‖ the "coat of mail" (i. 56, 3), "golden breastplates" (iv. 53, 4), "cuirasses of leather" (v. 5, 38), "cotton-quilted cuirass," "golden cuirass" (iv. 54, 11), "iron mail

* *Ṛig*-veda, i. 92, 4.

† Ibid, iii. 185.

‡ Ibid, i. 175; i. 64, 9.

§ Ibid, i. 94.

‖ Ibid, i. 25, 10, 13; v. 7, 25.

and armour." The *Rig*-veda notices banners (i. 103, 11); and the war-cry is also alluded to (i. 37, 2). The conch-shell in battle is mentioned (i. 112, 1). The drum* was the instrument for marshalling troops or giving orders to them. The martial wind instrument is also mentioned.† The army consisted of both foot soldiers (A. V. vii. 62, 1) and mounted troops. We read of "people arrayed in martial order" (v. 79, 2); and of the commander of the whole host (i. 33, 3). There were also messengers of war (iv. 83, 3). Warriors burnished their weapons (i. 92, 1); and they gained booty from their foes in battles (i. 73, 5). We read of arrows furnished with feathers, the horns of the deer forming their points (v. 75, 11). But arrows were generally made of the *sara* reed with a blade of iron and besmeared with poison (i. 117, 16). Their weapons and implements were swords, spears, lances, helmets, javelins, war-missiles, discuses, clubs, bucklers, bows, quivers, arrows, shafts, axes, razors, scissors, knives, hatchets, and hooks; and those that were made of metal were sharpened on grindstones (ii. 39, 7).

Religion moulded Indian life, and all its social and political institutions. Even investigations in the various departments of knowledge are traceable to religion. Astronomical observations were first carried on simply with a view to fix the right time for the performance of the sacrifices; and the earliest beginnings of geometrical and mathematical investigations among them arose also from certain sacrificial requirements. The laws of phonetics were cultivated because

* *Rig*-veda, i. 28, 5; vi. 47, 29, 31.

† Ibid, i. 117, 21.

it was a grave offence to the gods to pronounce wrongly a single letter of the sacrificial formulas; grammar and etymology were studied simply for the right understanding of the holy scriptures. And philosophy and theology have ever been closely connected.

They counted beyond a hundred.* The *Sulva-sûtras* of Baudhâyana and of A'pastamba, and the *Sulva-parisishta* of Kâtyâyana contain a number of interesting rules for the construction of the various altars, which could not be done without some amount of geometrical knowledge. The property of the right-angled triangle was known to them. They also tried to express the relation between the diagonal and the side of a square, and arrived at a very close approximation. But the most interesting attempt they made in the cultivation of geometrical operations was that of squaring the circle.

The mention of the "star-gazers,"† of the "calculator,"‡ of "observers of the stars," and "the science of astronomy,"§ warrants us to conclude that astronomical science was then actively cultivated. The quinquennial cycle|| as well as a sexennial cycle** was known to them; and the division of the year was made into twelve (or 13, i. e., the intercalary month††) months consisting of 360 days, and each day hav-

* White Yajur-veda, xvii.

† Ibid, v. 10.

‡ Ibid, v. 20.

§ Weber's History of Indian Literature, p. 30.

|| White Yajur-veda, v. 15; xxvii. 45; see also the *Rig-veda*, iii. 55, 18; i. 25, 8.

** Taittirîya-Brâhmana, iii. 10, 4, 1.

†† *Rig-veda*, i. 2.

ing 30 muhûrtas. The moon was to them the measurer of time ; and there is apparently an expression of an astronomical fact that she shines only through reflecting the light of the sun. They knew that "the sun does never set nor rise."* A close observation of the moon's progress, and of the appearance of the group of stars near which she passed, was already made. They had also the conception of the use of the lunar and solar years ; and of the method of adjusting them with reference to each other.† And they determined the cardinal points of the horizon (i. 31, 14) ; and calculated the eclipses.‡ It was also known to them that the earth turns regularly round the sun, whence it derives light and heat.§ They also divided the year into seasons.|| It is an interesting fact that they had some knowledge even of the laws of attraction ;** and it is not improbable that the law of gravitation may have been one of those known to them.

We read of the constellations ;†† and the Lunar Mansions (the Lunar Zodiac) comprise a division of the circle of the heavens into 27 equal parts of 13° 20′ to each part. It is to be understood that this division could not have been made without an instrument. Our ancestors must have possessed a knowledge of the use of appropriate apparatus like the armillary sphere to explain the lunar zodiac,

* Haug's Aitareya-Brâhmana, ii, p, 242.

† *Rig*-veda, i. 25, 8,

‡ Ibid, iv. 2, 12.

§ Yajur-veda, xx. 23.

|| *Rig*-veda, i. 95, 3.

** Ibid, ix. 86-19,

†† Ibid, i. 50, 2.

and to illustrate its use. The division of the heavens into twenty-seven Nakshatras, a division which is the soul of the sacred calendar, and according to which all the Vaidik sacrifices were performed,* is said not to have been indigenous in India, but borrowed from without. M. Biot published several articles in the Journal des Savans, in which he tried to prove the Chinese origin of the Indian Nakshatras. He maintained that the number of the Nakshatras was originally 28, and afterwards reduced to 27. There occurs one allusion to these Nakshatras in the Veda;† and the 27 divisions with their asterisms and presiding deities are spoken of in the Brâhma*nas*. But notwithstanding these facts it has been urged that the division of the heavens into 27 Nakshatras was borrowed from China. The originality of the Veda is certainly destroyed, in case it is proved that even at that early age a foreign civilization exercised influence upon the growth of the Indian mind. M. Biot supported his favorite propositions with so much learning and skill that so ingenious a scholar as Prof. Lassen took his side, and admitted the introduction of the Chinese *Sieu* into northern India before the 14th century B. C.‡ According to M. Biot's own statement the number of the Chinese *Sieu* was only 24, and was not raised to 28 till the year 1100 B. C. Astronomy, at least that portion of it, which bears relation to the Nakshatras, or the twenty-seven lunar mansions of the Indo-Aryans, is closely connected with the Vaidik worship.

The Vaidik sacrifices could not have been in any case performed without a knowledge of the lunar mansions. The

* *Ri*g-veda, x. 85, 2. † Haug's Aitareya-Brâhma*n*a, i. pp. 42 sq.

‡ Indian Antiquities, p. 747.

Indian names of the months were derived from the names of the constellations; and the names of the constellations again were derived, for the most part, from the names of ancient Vaidik deities.* The exact time of the lunar festivals is fixed with such close accuracy, that the Indo-Aryans, at the time when those public sacrifices were common, must have been, in a high degree, proficient in astronomy. The growth of astronomical knowledge in India, is closely connected with the intellectual and especially the religious history of that country. The original division of the year into lunar months must have taken effect prior to the first separation of the great Aryan family. If we find the same names of the months in Sanskrit and Chinese; and if these names the Chinese Dictionary cannot explain, surely the conclusion must be that they were borrowed by the Chinese from the Indo-Aryans, and not by the Indo-Aryans from the Chinese. The three winter months are designated in Chinese as Pehoua, Mokué, and Pholkuna; and these names correspond with the three Indian months Pausha, Mâgha, and Phâlguna. These Indian months received their names from the corresponding Nakshatras Pushyâ, Maghâ, and Phalgunî. Shall we infer, then, that the Indo-Aryans borrowed the idea of the lunar Nakshatras from the Chinese, or that the Chinese borrowed them from the Indo-Aryans? The Nakshatras were indeed suggested to the Indo-Aryans by the moon's sidereal revolution; and their number was originally 27 and not 28. The *Sieu* were originally 24 in number; and they were afterwards raised to 28. It must be observed here that there is no

* Whitney's Sûrya-Siddhânta, p. 203.

trace to be found of a like change in India. The *manâzel* of the Arabians were also directly derived from India. The Chinese system of *Sieu* differs from the Indian system of Nakshatras both in its structure and its object. The object of the Nakshatra system was to mark the progress of the sun, the moon, and the planets through the heavens. This Nakshatra system had from the beginning a strictly scientific structure and application. The relation of the Chinese *Sieu* to the Nakshatras, is altogether out of the question. The *Sieu* throughout are but single stars;* while the *Târâs* are clusters of stars. The attempt to identify the Chinese *Sieu* with the Indian Nakshatras, or 27 lunar mansions, is decidedly futile.

Another proof of the social progress of the Indo-Aryans is derived from their knowledge of herbs and mode of medical treatment. There is mention made of medicaments for the ailments of our bodies (v. 74, 3); and a hymnist prays to Rudra saying "Invigorate our sons by thy medical plants" (ii. 33, 4). "Ambrosia," says a son of Kanva, "is in the waters." "All medicaments are in the waters" (i. 23, 20), thus anticipating in so remote antiquity the hydropathic doctrine of the present century. They had the knowledge of the three humours of the body, *i. e.*, wind, bile, and phlegm (i. 34, 6); and of the hygienic properties of water, air, and vegetables. Agni is said to be the remover of diseases. The Asvins are called physicians of the gods; and they are said to have given sight to Kanva.† Soma is also supposed to preside over medicinal herbs. Anatomi-

* Whitney's Sûrya-Siddhânta, p. 207.

† Rig-veda, i. 117.

cal observations were then simply made by dissecting the victims at the sacrifices. At any rate animal anatomy was perfectly understood, as each of the different parts of the body had its own well-defined name.* There is ample evidence of the practice of medicine in those early days; and we read of a "doctor who seeks a patient."

* Weber's History of Indian Literature, p. 30.

CHAPTER II.

Vaidik Theogony and Mythology—Abstract Conceptions of the Deity—Cosmogony—Vaidik Doctrine of a Future Life—Priesthood and Vaidik Ceremonials of Worship.

THERE is a faculty of faith in man, a power independent of sense and reason, and the primordial source of any religion, which enables him to apprehend the Infinite. In the hymns we hear in unmistakable language the lispings of infancy, the groanings of struggling spirits for something that is neither conceivable or utterable. And in such mental struggles they formed various conceptions of the deity; and as the case may be, they also made no apparent distinction between the concrete and the abstract, nor between the material and the spiritual. In the first stage of thought when the mind had not risen to the conception of the unity of God, it was but natural that the principal powers of nature should at first draw the attention of man; and thus the sun, the moon and other bright objects would be worshipped and adored as they appeared to possess unbounded powers; and that the different domains of nature should be allotted to different gods, each of whom presided over his own province. But in the *Rig-veda* such departments are not clearly defined; and we thus see that one domain was presided over by more than one deity.* The flaming orb of the mighty brilliant sun, thunderstorm, flashing lightnings, rolling thunders, furious blasts, rain, mists, and hail made a tremendous impression upon the desponding minds of our ancestors. The mind of man when so simple and childlike begins to reflect upon the powerful and unintelligible forces of nature, and being bewildered in its own ignorance, in awe bows down and offers sacrifices to them. It represents them sometimes as benevolent, and sometimes as terrible; and ascribes to them the very same character which it observes in daily life. Such was the natural working of the minds of our ancestors in the childhood of their faith. The birth of certain gods is even conceived; and such birth can have no other than a physical meaning.† But the general absence of anthropomorphism from the Vaidik notions of divine beings is conspicuous.‡ The real theogony of the Veda is not the

* Muir's Original Sanskrit Texts, v. p. 5.

‡ Müller's Chips from a German Workshop, i. p. 38.

‡ "The Vedas hold out precautions against framing a Deity after human imagination, and recommend mankind to direct all researches towards the surrounding objects, viewed, either collectively or individually, bearing in mind their regular, wise, and wonderful combinations and arrangements."—*Introduction to the Abridgment of the Vedânta by Raja Rammohun Roy, p. vii.* Max Müller, in his Chips from a German Workshop, i. p. 38, says, "The religion of the Veda knows of no idols. The worship of idols in India is a secondary formation, a later degradation of the more primitive worship of ideal gods." Dr. Bollensen, in the Journal of the German Oriental Society, xxii. pp. 587ff., on the other hand, contends against this opinion. When we take into consideration the fact that our

property of the Indo-Aryans alone ; but the joint-property of the whole Aryan race. The mythology of the *Ri*g-veda is sometimes very marked and distinct, and sometimes very indistinct and hazy. But, no doubt, there is more distinct mythology in the ninth and tenth books than in the first eight books of the Veda. The mythology of one *Ri*shi is not necessarily the mythology of others ; and as there are many *Ri*shis, so there are many mythologies. Max Müller has attempted to explain the Vaidik mythology by propounding the solar theory ; and Kuhn the meteorological theory. According to the former the Aryans, as they were highly imaginative, gave various names to the same object ; but they soon forgot the importance or rather the import of the original name, and consequently mythology arose. The origin of almost all mythological legends is solely attributable to the naïve ascription of human agency to other beings and also to animate things, and consequently to their ultimate individualization. However it was the first stage in the growth of Vaidik mythology ; but language was never at rest to spin it. It has been very appropriately said that mythology was the bane of the ancient world, a disease of language.* It is never-

ancestors were of a deep poetical temperament and of a delicate imaginative nature, it appears very probable that the gods received a variety of ideal or human forms and epithets. Thus they were invoked to discharge the functions which the poetical feeling of their worshippers attributed to them. Hence when we read of such epithets as n*ri*pesas (*Ri*g-veda, iii. 4, 5) &c., and of such expressions as rûpa, vapus, and sand*ri*s, we are to understand them as used only in a metaphorical sense. See on this subject Prof. Williams' Indian Wisdom, p. 15.

* Müller's Lectures on the Science of Language, i. p. 11.

theless history changed into fable; which is not without peculiar charms and which is also full of interesting problems that supply ample materials for the history of Aryan thought. And it is at the same time most valuable to the student of history not only in a philological, but also a philosophical, and more especially a psychological point of view.

Yâska, following the ancient expounders who preceded him, has reduced the number of the gods to three, viz., Agni whose place is on the earth; Vâyu, or Indra, whose place is in the atmosphere; and Sûrya whose place is in the sky.* Besides this triple classification the gods are sometimes said to be thirty-three in number;† and sometimes as being much more numerous, i. e., three hundred, three thousand and thirty-nine.‡ They are again divided into great and small, young and old.§ But this distinction is denied in another passage;‖ and though frequently described as immortal,** they are never spoken of as self-existent beings.

Dyaus, or the Greek Zeus, and Prithivî are invoked to attend religious rites; and to grant a variety of boons. They are described as possessing physical, moral and spiritual characteristics. They are jointly called parents;

* Nirukta, vii. 5., and compare *Rig*-veda, x. 158, 1.

† *Rig*-veda, i. 34, 11; i. 45, 2; i. 139, 11; viii. 28, 1; viii. 30, 2; viii. 35, 3; ix. 92, 4; and compare *Satapatha-Brâhmana*, iv. 5, 7, 2.

‡ *Rig*-veda, iii. 9, 9.

§ Ibid, i. 27, 13.

‖ Ibid, viii. 30, 1.

** Ibid, i. 24, 1; i. 72, 2, 10; i. 189, 3; iii. 21, 1; iv. 42, 1; x. 13, 1; x. 69, 9.

but elsewhere the Heaven is singly called father and the Earth mother. They are the parents of not only men but of the gods also. They are said to be the creators and sustainers of all things; but passages are not wholly wanting where they are spoken of as themselves created. Though Indra is said to be their creator; yet they are also spoken of as created by Soma, Pûshan, Dhâtri and Hiranyagarbha. They are also said to have received their shape from Tvashtri, and to have sprung from the head and feet of Purusha; and to be supported by Mitra, Savitri, Varuna, Indra, Soma and Hiranyagarbha.

Aditi is the only goddess spoken of by name in the *Rig*-veda. What is not Diti is Aditi. She is styled the goddess or the divine; and is the source and supporter of all things, and represents the whole nature. She is supplicated for different blessings, and for forgiveness of sins. She is said to be the mother of Varuna and of other gods;* and her gifts are pure and celestial. She, as the great power, wields the forces of the universe, and controls men by moral laws. In the Sâma-veda Aditi is represented with her sons and brothers. The sons are styled A'dityas; and they are Mitra, Aryaman, Bhaga, Varuna, Daksha and Amsa.† But in some places they are stated to be seven, in others eight in number, though their names are not given there. They are described as sleepless, many-eyed, vast, strong, bright, holy, pure, golden, sinless, blameless. They are far-observing; and all things

* M. Ad. Regnier, E'tude sur l'idiomè des Vedas, p. 28.

† *Rig*-veda, ii. 27, 1.

are near to them. They see good and evil in men's hearts, and punish sin.

Mitra is frequently associated with Varuna. Varuna, however, is sometimes separately celebrated; Mitra but seldom. Mitra etymologically signifying *measurer*, was originally the name of the day; and Varuna etymologically signifying *coverer*, was originally the name of the night. Mitra and Varuna are the most important from the identification of the former with the Mithra of the Zand-Avesta;* and of the latter with the Uranos of the Greeks. Varuna occupies a rather more prominent place in the hymns; he presides over light, and it is said in one passage that the constellations are his holy acts, and that the moon moves by his command. He is called the source of light; he grants wealth, averts evil, and protects cattle. In another passage, he is said to abide in the ocean, and to be acquainted with the course of ships. He is also said to know the flight of birds in the sky, and the regular succession of months. His character does not, however, appear to have been the same throughout the whole period represented by the Vaidik hymns. He is the sovereign of his own abode; and a king both of the gods and of men often surrounded by his messengers. He is mighty, fixed in purpose, far-sighted and visible to his worshippers. To him are attributed the grandest cosmical

* Herodotus confounds Mitra with Mylitha; but the important thing to be observed is, that Mitra was a Persian god. There are evidently many passages in the Vendîdâd which prove that among the ancient Persians Mithra was sometimes represented as the Sun. But the modern Pârsis understand by it Meher Izad, in contradistinction to Khurbeshid, the Sun.

functions. He is said to have created the Heaven and the Earth; and to uphold, and rule over them. He possesses high moral character more than any other gods. His laws are fixed and unimpeachable; and he controls the destinies of men. He is besought to drive away evil, to give deliverance from sin, and to prolong life. The same attributes and functions are also ascribed to Mitra. Varuna was an older god than Indra; and the homage originally paid to the former was gradually transferred to the latter. The Varuna-worship declined, and the Indra-worship superseded it. This was the result of the gradual change which marked the Indo-Aryan religion. The anteriority of Varuna to Indra is borne out by the coincidence of his name with the Uranos of the Greek mythology; while all attempts at the identification of Indra with any other character of the same mythology are out of the question.

Indra was human; he is reputed as the destroyer of Vritra, an Asura or Assyrian. His original name was Ind. He was deified for his exploits. He is described as being born; and as having both parents. He is also said to have been produced by the gods; and to have sprung from the mouth of Purusha. He is a twin brother of Agni. The highest divine attributes and functions are attributed to him. He is spoken of in some places as having physical superiority; and in others as having no spiritual elevation or moral grandeur; though there are various other texts in which he is found to be invested with ethical character. He is besought by men like a father, and for temporal blessings; and even faith in him is enjoined. He is represented as heroic, strong, martial, ancient, youthful, undecaying and wielding the thunderbolt. He is golden; and can assume any shape at will. His wife is alluded to; and his intimate relation with his worshippers is spoken of. He is the destroyer of enemies; and he conquered heaven by austerity.

Vâyu, the blower, is frequently found in conjunction with Indra; and does not seem to occupy a very prominent place in the *R*ig-veda. He is the son-in-law of Tvash*tri*; and is spoken of as beautiful in form. Pûshan nourished the growth of crops. He is the protector on a journey, particularly of robbers; and he is said to be the divinity presiding over the earth. He is connected with the marriage ceremonial (x. 85, 26 and 37); and is supplicated to take the bride's hand and lead her away, and to bless her in her conjugal relation. Rudra literally means one who cries; and in process of time he became the god of thunder. The character of Rudra is identical with that of Pûshan. He is the source of fertility, and the giver of happiness; and he is said to preside over medicinal plants, and is invoked for the removal of diseases. He is represented as the lord of evil spirits. He was originally an object of worship with the aborigines; and such worship was gradually adopted by the Indo-Aryans. The Maruts, the pounders, or Rudras are the sons of Rudra and P*ri*sni. They are very commonly represented as the attendants of Indra, and as the children of the ocean. They are spoken of as golden-footed; and they are said to worship Indra. The Maruts were the leaders of hunters; but in course of time they seem to have lost their anthropopathic character. The invocations of the Visve-devâ*h* or the *All-gods* as they are called, represent a later phase of thought than the invocations of each individual deity singly. They are nine in number, such as Indra, Agni, Mitra, Varu*n*a and the rest. They are besought as preservers of men, and as bestowers of rewards.

Agni (is identical with the Latin Ignis) is indeed called the lowest of the gods, but notwithstanding this he is greatly revered. He is invoked at all sacrifices; and as he is the sacrificial fire, he is the servant of both men and of the gods, carrying the invocations and the offerings of the former to the latter; he invites the gods to the ceremonies; and performs them in behalf of the lord of the house. Represented as a divinity, his is immortality, his is never-failing youth, invested with infinite power and glory. He is the granter of life, health, food, wealth and cattle. He is the source of effulgent light, and the destroyer of all things. He is golden-haired and an emblem of purity. He is known under various appellations; and many deities inferior to him are purely his manifestations. He is identified with Vish*n*u, Varu*n*a, Mitra, Indra, Aryaman, Yama, A*ms*a, Tvash*t*ri, Rudra, Pûshan, Savit*r*i, Bhaga, Aditi, Hotrâ, Bhâratî, I*l*â, Sarasvatî, and with the eternal Vedhas; and the functions and attributes of other deities are often ascribed to him. He is the son of the Heaven and the Earth; and elsewhere he is said to have been generated by the gods, and to have been brought from the sky by Mâtari*s*van. His production is also attributed to the waters. He again is the father of the gods; and is regarded as having a triple existence. He knows the races of the gods and of men. He is the protector, friend, and leader of the people. He is the divine king, and is as strong as Indra; and is worshipped by Varuna, Mitra, the Maruts, and all the three thousand, three hundred and thirty-nine gods.

Sûrya, or the Greek Helios, and Savitri are exact personifications of the sun; and under these two different epithets the sun is chiefly representd in the hymns. Sûrya is spoken of as an A'ditya; and occupies in the Vaidik worship a place not so prominent as could be naturally anticipated from the magnificence and splendour of that luminous body. He is said to be god-born, and to have been generated by Indra, Agni, Soma, Mitra, and Varuna. He is the divine leader or the priest of the gods. Like Agni and Indra, he is the source of light, and the granter of temporal blessings. He is all-seeing; and he beholds the good and bad deeds of the mortals. He is said to be the healer of leprosy. Only three *sûktas* in the first book of the Rig-veda are addressed to him; and these "convey no very strikingly expressive acknowledgment of his supremacy." Although the Sun-worship was not prominent, the Indo-Aryans loved light and even warmth, and the sun or the "ray diffuser." The expressions contained in the hymns relating to this deity exhibit a careful and loving observation of Nature. He is spoken of as coming "from a distance," and "removing all sins;" or as the divine Sun he is supplicated to take away the "sickness of the heart," and the "yellowness of the body,"

Savitri, who was originally the autumnal sun, is sometimes distinguished from Sûrya; and is frequently identified with Mitra and Pûshan. He is the golden deity, yellow-haired, golden-handed, and golden-tongued. He is the bestower of all desirable things; and confers blessings from the sky, from the atmosphere, and from the earth. He is said to have bestowed immortality on the gods.

The Asvins are in various texts connected with Sûrya. They are the twin sons of Vivasvat and Sara*n*yû; and are also called the sons of the sky. They are described as young, beautiful, ancient, strong, bright, terrible, and skilful. They bestow food and wealth. They ever occupy themselves with multifarious earthly transactions, enable the worshippers to baffle their enemies, assist them in their need, and extricate them from difficulty. Their business is more earthly than heavenly. They cure the blind, the lame, the emaciated, and the sick. They are besought for different blessings; for long life, offspring, wealth, victory, destruction of enemies, and forgiveness of sins. The myth of the human Asvins has two distinct elements, one cosmical and the other human or historical; which have in course of time become blended into one. The cosmical element refers to their luminous nature; and the human element to the wonderful cures effected by them. They were probably some renowned mortals, horsemen of celebrity, who were admitted on account of their wonderful medical skill to the companionship of the gods.

Tvash*t*ri (the Vulcan) is frequently found connected with the *R*ibhus. He is the divine artisan, the skilful worker, and the creator of all forms. He is also versed in all magical devices. He forges the thunderbolts of Indra. He bestows long life, offspring, wealth and protection; and forms husband and wife for each other. He is supplicated to preserve the worshippers. He was also a renowned mortal; and as the skilful artisan he had been translated into the companionship of the gods.

Soma is the god who plays an important part in the sacrificial act of the Vaidik age. He is said to be divine, and the soul of sacrifice. He is the king of the gods and of men. He is the lord of creatures; and the generator of the sky and earth, of Agni, Sûrya, Indra and Vishnu. He is wise, strong, agile, and thousand-eyed. He beholds all the worlds, and destroys the irreligious. He is immortal, and confers immortality on the gods and on men. He is generous as a father to a son; and is supplicated to forgive sins. In the post-Vaidik age the name Soma came to be commonly applied to the moon and its regent. Even in the *Rig*-veda some traces of this application seem to be discoverable.*

The connexion of the personified Dawn or Ushas (the Aurora of the Latins) with Sûrya makes its worship a form of solar adoration. The hymns put up to her, are not wrapped up in mystic language or fantastic allegory. The invigorating influence which the dawn exercises on both the body and the mind; and the luminous and other pleasant phenomena connected with day-break, constitute the subject of some of the best portions of Vaidik poetry; and out of them the conceptions of Ushas arose. She is invoked as the affluent, as the

* x. 85, 2 ff; and compare, "The transference of the name Soma to the moon, which appears in the later history of the Indian religion, is hitherto obscure: the Vedas hardly know it, nor do they seem to prepare the way for it in any manner."—Whitney's Oriental and Linguistic Studies, p. 11.

giver of food, and bringer of opulence; she is asked to lavish on the pious riches, horses, cattle, posterity, and troops of slaves ; and she is praised for the numerous and various boons she bestowed on the worshippers who were liberal to her. She is the goddess imbued with an excellent intellect, is truthful, and the fulfiller of her promises. She invigorates the diligent; when she appears, bipeds and quadrupeds are in motion; the winged birds hover in the air ; and men who have to earn their bread quit their homes. She rides, in a golden chariot, which is large and beautiful. The relation of Ushas to other Vaidik deities is two-fold, physical and ritual, in as much as the phenomena of the dawn are associated with the other phenomena of Nature, and as certain religious ceremonies are held at the beginning of the day. For this, she is frequently addressed as the daughter of the Heaven; and when her parents are spoken of, the commentators explain this word as signifying the Heaven and the Earth. She is further called the daughter of the night ; but, on other grounds, she is also described as having Night for her sister. Besides, she is the sister of Bhaga, the kinswoman of Varu*n*a, and the faithful wife of Sûrya.

Parjanya or Perkunas* is the thundering rain-god. He appears to have been associated with Vâta, the blast, and Agni ; but was decidedly distinct from Indra. He is called the son of Dyaus, and the father of the Soma plant. He is represented as the lord of all moving creatures.

* Benfey's Orient und Occident, i. p. 214.

He presides over the lightning, thunder, and rain; and is said to impregnate the plants.

Brahma*n*aspati or B*r*ihaspati is described as the offspring of the two Worlds. He appears sometimes to be identical with Indra; but is elsewhere distinguished from Agni. He is styled the father of the gods; and is possessed of all divine attributes. He is bright, pure, clear-voiced, opulent, and a remover of diseases. He is called a priest; and intercedes with the gods on behalf of men. He is the protector of the pious; and saves them from all dangers.

Trita A'ptya, Ahirbudhnya, and Aja Ekapâd are minor divinities. Trita is conjoined with the Maruts, with Vâta or Vâyu, and Indra. He is called A'ptya; and his abode is hidden. He bestows long life. Ahirbudhnya is the Dragon of the deep; and resides in the atmospheric ocean. Aja Ekapâd is probably a storm-god.

Sarasvatî is a goddess of some importance in the *R*igveda. She is celebrated both as a river and as a deity. She was indeed primarily a river-deity. She bestows prosperity, wealth, offspring and fertility. She attends the sacrifices along with other goddesses, Bhâratî Hotrâ, Varûtrî, Mahî, I*l*â, Dhisha*n*â. Ara*n*yâ*n*î is mentioned as the goddess of forest solitude. Anumati or "the moon one digit less than full," Râkâ, or "the full moon," Sinîvâlî, or "the last day before the new moon," and Kuhû or Gungû, or "the new moon," are some other goddesses represented in the hymns. Râkâ is closely connected with parturition. *S*raddhâ is an object of adoration in the morning, at noon, and at sunset. She is the personification of an abstract idea or religious faith. She prospers the liberal worshippers of the gods, and imparts faith. Lakshmî and *S*rî do not occur in the hymns in the sense as they appear in the later mythology. *S*rî is mentioned as issuing forth from Prajâpati when he was wrapped up in intense austerity. Aditi, the mother of the A'dityas, is the representative of the universe ; Diti her counterpart. Nish*t*igrî is the mother, and Indrâ*n*î the wife, of Indra. P*ri*s*n*i is the mother of the Maruts. Sûryâ is the daughter of the sun, and the spouse of the A*s*vins, or of Soma. Besides these goddesses a few others, such as Agnâyî, Varu*n*ânî, Rodasî, and Aramati are also celebrated in the hymns of the *R*ig-veda.

No reference to tangible things as objects of worship has been discovered in the old hymns. But with regard to semi-tangible and intangible objects, the case is really very different.* Most of the gods are merely poetical names, names denoting purely sensuous objects ; which gradually assumed a divine personality of course never thought of by the original authors. These names no doubt had originally their material meaning ; but gradually they came to be used in the spiritual sense. They again were sometimes used merely as appellatives ; and sometimes as names of gods. It is thus seen that many names were created owing to the utter helplessness of the worshippers to express their ideas of the deity. Indeed, names after names were created to express the infinity and the majesty of the divine ; and this was only suggested by the consciousness of the insufficiency of those names that had been already created and used to convey such ideas.

* Müller's Hibbert Lectures, p. 198.

However, every name was created with a distinct purpose; and so had a history full of useful lessons. And in fact an idea of a deity under such varying disguises evinces a great progress of thought. It is thus clear that the idea of God existed in a vague and hazy form; who was not yet defined or properly named. The names given to God gradually came to signify distinct divinities. There may be error in all those names; but the simple attempt to give a name was the greatest triumph of the adoring poets; who had a longing for God, who felt kinship between themselves and God,* and who invented names after names to grasp and comprehend him. A name, however, is not a mere name, not a hollow phraseology, it is not mute, but has life in it. And in such names there must have been, as it were, some presentiments of monotheism. The hymns were composed neither in the same age, nor by the same poet, nor did they originate at the same localities, nor under the same circumstances. They are the work of many *R*ishis and of many centuries. There could be found, therefore, neither much consistency of thought nor of idea in them. As the conceptions of the different poets could be various, so the natures of the gods must have differintiated. The same god is represented in one hymn as supreme and equal; and again in others as inferior. There are also many passages in which the attributes of infinity, omnipotence, and omnipresence are ascribed to each of the gods.† However, the whole nature of these

* *R*ig-veda,, ii. 11, 12; viii. 47, 8; viii. 82, 32; x. 142, ..

† *R*ig-veda, x, 90, 1 ff; x. 121, 1 ff.

ideal and imaginary gods is still transparent; they are merely names of natural phenomena and are without being; they are the creatures of man and not his creators. Here names play with us. The consciousness that all the deities are but different names of one and the same godhead is manifest in some of the hymns of the Veda. In one hymn it is distinctly stated that the gods, though differently named and represented, are really one and the same; but men call them by different names, and the poets represent the one and the same god in different forms:—"They call him Indra, Mitra, Varu*n*a, Agni; and (he is) the well-winged, celestial Garutmat. Sages name variously that which is but one:–they call it Agni, Yama, Mâtari*s*van."* Savit*r*i is the supporter of the sky and the lord of creatures.† Varu*n*a is said to be the lord of all, of gods and men, of heaven and earth.‡ Indra is also clearly conceived as the supreme god;§ and as regards the character and functions of Tvash*t*ri we have an approach to the idea of a supreme creator of the universe. According to the Taittirîya-Brâhma*n*a the gods attained their divine rank by austerity.‖ They are said to possess in an eminent degree the qualities of the *R*ishis; and so they are also styled Kavi, *R*ishi, etc.¶ This possibly implies that the

* *R*ig-veda, i. 164, 46; see also Colebrooke's Essay, i. 26 f.; Weber's Indische Studien, v. p. iv.

† Ibid, iv. 53, 2.

‡ Ibid, i. 25, 20; ii. 27, 10.

§ Ibid, vii. 32.

‖ Muir's Original Sanskrit Texts, iii. p. 276.

¶ *R*ig-veda, v. 29, 1; vi. 14, 2; viii, 6, 41; viii. 16, 7; ix. 96, 18; ix. 107, 7; x. 27, 22; x. 112, 9.

*R*ishis thought they possessed particular knowledge of the deities, with whom they believed they had an affinity. "Indeed, the relations between the Vaidik Aryans and their deities appear to have been of a childlike and filial character; the evils which they suffered, they ascribed to some offence of omission or commission which had been given to a deity; whilst the good which they received was in like manner ascribed to his kindness and favor."* The deities of the primitive Vaidik times represented not only the conspicuous processes of external nature; but also the higher relations of moral and social life. The songs with which the Indo-Aryans invoked the gods clearly show that they sought them for their spiritual as well as for their material welfare. Ethical considerations are not, therefore, extraneous to these instinctive outbursts of the pious mind. The distinction between good and bad was made in a moral sense; and law and virtue were also recognised.† Sin and evil, indeed, are often adverted to; and the gods are extolled because they destroy sinners and evil-doers.‡ Even the idea of personal sin is to be met with in the Black Yajus. "May our sins be removed" or "repented of" is the burden of several hymns in the *R*ik (i, 97; ii. 24, 5; ii. 33, 6; vii. 32, 9; viii. 13, 15); and there is only one other hymn in which the hymnist prays to be absolved not only from his own sins but also from the sins of his fathers (vii. 86). It is not so diffi-

* Wheeler's History of India. i. p. 13.

† *R*ig-veda, ii. 28, 5; ii. 29, 1.

‡ Ibid, i. 35, 3, 11; i. 36, 14; i. 115, 6; ii. 27, 14; and see also Johnson's Oriental Religions, p. 119.

cult now to have the idea as to the writers' notion of sin or of repentance when it is an undeniable fact that they distinctly acknowledged two eternal principles of Good and Evil. The two ideas of justice and mercy are also to be met with in the hymns.* However, there are to be found many hymns in the *Rik* which depart materially from the simplicity of the conceptions here alluded to.

Our Aryan ancestors carried with them their religion and worship when they started from their primitive home, and spread themselves over the various parts of the world. Therefore, among different branches of the family there is to be found a great harmony which subsisted in their original worship and in the names of God and of the gods. Indeed, the Indo-Aryans, Greeks, Romans, Germans, Celtics at one time worshipped the same gods. Although Indo-Aryan mythology is extravagant and ridiculous, and has an icy coldness of meaning in it, yet those mythological dreams have an enduring symbolic value, and stand as data for primitive history. The Indo-Aryans early speculated largely on matters supernatural ; and their religion was an important feature of their civilization. The Vaidik religion in all its aspects is the true expression of the view which our simple-minded but highly gifted ancestors imbued with deep religious feelings, took of the wonderful powers and phenomena of nature. And there is no doubt that it originated in the minds of single individuals, whether inspired or not inspired ; but this cannot be said of the whole

* Müller's Chips from a German Workshop, p. 39.

body of the people. In the hymns there is a deep awakening of the religious sentiment, and a sense of the divine. In all the objects of nature our ancestors beheld either the primary causes of them, or the visible emblems of the invisible great cause. But once the religious faculty being roused, the human mind, which is subtle introversive and contemplative, could never be satisfied with the mere idea that the elements are the sole causes of creation; and so it must go on to spiritualize the gigantic forms of nature by which we are surrounded; and as to the extent to which the beautiful conceptions of poetic fancy are carried, religion must of necessity become fetchism, pantheism, or polytheism. And polytheism can only be the result when each spirit is allowed to assume a separate form, and is invested with attributes as worthy as could be of its emblem. In the oldest portions of the hymns, there are few traces to be found of abstract conceptions of the deity. They apparently disclose the primitive stage of religious belief of simple men; who, under the influence of the most wonderful phenomena of nature, felt every where the presence and agency of divine powers; and who had not then risen to a clear idea of one Supreme God. Our ancestors imagined that each of the provinces of the universe was controlled and regulated by each of the deities; and this is clearly shown by the special functions assigned to them, and by the very names under which they are designated.

The Vedas contain no real system; they never classify or define the objects of worship. This was, however, done at last by commentators, who seem to have generally misunderstood the religion taught in them. Every object in the universe awed our earliest forefathers and roused them from stolid wonderment to think and ponder; and thus in the childhood of their faith they looked for the infinite in the moon and the sun, in the sky, in the storm, and in a flash of lightning. And so they called it at one time wielder of thunderbolt, giver of rain, bringer of light, thunderer, bestower of food and life; and at last creator, preserver, ruler, king, father, and god of gods. All this we see in one great evolution of religious thought, as no concept is possible without a name. All that we see is that they felt the presence of God in every object they beheld in the universe; and that they tried to rise from Nature up to Nature's God. However, it is really impossible to give a name to the religion of the *R*ishis. They used words which are always extremely important, both psychologically and historically. But we cannot use them now in their etymological meaning nor in the senses which must have passed at one time through an historical evolution. Faith, worship, hope and reverence for the gods—all this was religion to them. But we cannot characterise the ancient Vaidik religion as Henotheism or Kathenotheism; it is impossible to give a general name for it. There are numerous passages in the *R*ig-veda in many of which a monotheistic and in many others a pantheistic tendency is very clearly manifested. In the later stage of reflection our ancestors very possibly made approximations to monotheistic tendencies; and those approximations could only be weak and sporadic; and thus such a speculative monotheism was of necessity of a barren and shadowy character. In the hymns there are traces of human conceptions, human aspirations, human wisdom, and human folly. They have their material and spiritual aspect; they are at once vaguely pantheistic, severely monotheistic, grossly polytheistic, and coldly atheistic. They contain but the common principle of all the four. This prehistoric star-dust of all the systems may properly be called pantheism not in its exclusive sense. It is not philosophical abstraction but intense realisation. The polytheism of the Vedas like their pantheism is in the free, plastic age. The complicated polytheism which we find in the hymns is but the full development of polytheism of anterior centuries. It is evident that monotheism was never the starting point of the Vaidik system. We cannot conceive at the first stage of thought of the unity existing under the diversity; and such a conception as the first fruit of theosophic philosophy, is decidedly of later growth, and the result of subsequent reflection and comparison. We are therefore led to believe that monotheism never preceded polytheism. When the human spirit is once gifted with clear ideas of the unity of nature and of its Author, it is not possible that it should ignore that original cognition, and betake itself to the vagaries of naturalism and the worship of the multifarious deities of the proper Vaidik Olympus.

The ideas of entity and non-entity were very well familiar to the Vaidik *R*ishis.* In the 90th hymn of the tenth book of the *R*ig-veda the unity of the godhead is recog-

* *R*ig-veda, x. 72.

nised, although in a clearly pantheistic sense. We see elsewhere that the sun, the sky, and the earth were at one time considered as natural objects generated by the gods; and at another time as themselves the gods who created all things. Some scholars have gone so far as to assert that the idea of one God breaks through the mist of a polytheistic and an idolatrous phraseology. This is a mistake. The human mind in its natural operation strives to reduce all objects and events to unity and harmony, and to trace everything to a single source; and until there could be made a sufficient progress towards the knowledge of the unity and harmony of this marvellous universe, it is not possible for men to attain to a real conception of the unity of the Godhead. Oneness of god does not however exclude the idea of plurality of gods. There was no word yet to express the abstract idea of an immaterial and supernatural Being. The attributes of supremacy and omnipotence ascribed to one god did by no means exclude the admission of gods or names of gods. And it is also clear from the hymns that the poets never thought of other gods when they addressed their own god. But in some cases this idea is not admissible with the worship of two in the dual as Mitrâ-varu*n*au, Indrâ-somau, etc., or many in one group in the plural, as the Vi*s*ve-devâ*h* and the Maruts. The Vaidik hymns are, in one sense, both physiolatrous and polytheistic. The age when they were composed, as appears clearly from the Brâhma*n*as or directories for their use in the Brahma sacrifices, was followed by a palpable deterioration in the thought and feeling of the Indo-Aryans. At first the polytheism was simple. "The polytheistic idea, however, when once it had begun to work, would tend constantly to multiply the number of divinities, as we see it has already done in the Vaidik age."* There never was nor could be a pure polytheism or a pure monotheism. It is beyond doubt, that the human mind, in proportion to its power of observation and reflection, advances towards monotheism. But it is to be confessed that such movement is very slow, and often obstructed by tradition and habit. We must not place at the commencement that which ought to be placed at the very end. However, it is clear that our ancestors were polytheists before their separation ; and they could never completely forget what they once learnt and brought with them as a heritage from their original home. Such teaching, which again they had left as a legacy, had acted, upon the whole, most potently on the minds of their descendants from generation to generation ; until the proper philosophical age dawned, and the Upanishads were composed and their doctrines had taken ground. But the influence of such philosophical writings has been in no way complete nor permanent ; and their attempts towards obliteration at once from the mind, of the polytheistic principles, were far from being successful.

The Indo-Aryans had not attained to a clear and logical comprehension of the characteristics which they themselves ascribed to the objects of their worship. The conceptions of the Godhead indicated in the hymns are of a fluctuating and undecided character. The remarkable representations of a host of subordinate objects of worship, exhibit to us a conception of the universe by our

* Pictet's Origines Indo-Européennes, ii. pp. 708 ff.

ancestors which was mythical, sacramental, polytheistic, and even pantheistic. In the childhood of the world, the Indo-Aryans possessing simple and reflective minds solved the mysterious and difficult problem of the production of the existing universe in various ways. They entertained a great number of different conjectures with regard to cosmogony. As the case may be, they ascribed it sometimes to physical, and sometimes to spiritual powers. And as speculation gradually acquired vigour, different opinions asserted themselves, and they naturally became perplexed; and one of them asks: "What was the forest, what was the tree, out of which they fashioned heaven and earth? Inquire with your minds, ye sages, what was that on which he (Visvakarman) took his stand when supporting the world?"* Another poet asks, "Which of these two was the first, and which the last? How have they been produced? Sages, who knows?"† And as further speculations were carried on they gradually arrived at the idea of the universe having sprung out of darkness and a pre-existing chaos;‡ this notion could only have presented to them by the changes which constantly occurred before their eyes in the universe. And this

* *Rig*-veda, x. 81, 4; see also Taittirīya-Brâhmana, ii. 8, 9, 6.

† Ibid, i. 185, 1.

‡ Compare Genesis, i. 1. Here the meaning of the verb *barâ* is rendered by "created." But it simply conveys the sense of mere fashioning or arranging; and does by no means signify an *ex nihilo creation*. There is also no trace of the meaning attributed to it by later scholars of a creation out of nothing, According to the Jewish commentators it does not represent so. However, this idea is altogether a modern idea; and to transfer a modern idea to the mind of Moses is simply absurd.

doctrine is found to be propounded in one of the later hymns of the *R*ig-veda.* In different other hymns, however, we meet with various speculations about the origin of heaven and earth. The creation of them is sometimes ascribed to Indra, and at other times to other deities, such as Soma, Pûshan, Dhât*r*i and Hira*n*yagarbha. And it is also said that they have received their shape from Tvash*t*ri, and have sprung from the head and feet of Purusha; and are supported by Mitra, Varu*n*a, Indra, Agni, Savit*r*i and Soma. Elaborate theories of creation are not to be found in the earlier portions of the hymns;† and even the *R*ishis themselves apparently confess their ignorance of the beginning of all things.‡

There is a hymn in the tenth book of the *R*ig-veda of a long antecedent period, of philosophical thought in which we find the conception of a beginning of all things, and of a state, before all things were created. In the beginning there was nothing, no sky, no firmament. No space there was, no life, no time, no difference between day and night. "Darkness there was, and all at first was veiled in gloom profound, as ocean without light." There was only the deep abyss, a chaotic mass, which swallowed every thing. "That one," the poet says, "breathed, and lived; it enjoyed more than mere existence; yet its life was not dependent on any thing else, as our life depends on the air which we breathe. It breathed breathless." Max Müller says "language blushes at such expressions,

* *R*ig-veda, x. 129.

† Ibid, i. 67, 3; vii, 86, 1.

‡ Ibid, i. 164, 4; x. 81, 4.

but her blush is a blush of triumph." The creation is sometimes said to be the manifestation of His will; and a mere evolution of one substance. The idea of the spontaneous evolution of all things out of undeveloped matter, became the foundation of the Sânkhya philosophy. In that remote period we find that the difference between mind and matter was but imperfectly conceived.

The history of mankind clearly shows that man is essentially religious; and the belief in the unseen spiritual world has its foundation in our nature. The high-water marks of the radical elements of real religion, such as an intuition of God, a sense of human weakness and a feeling of dependence on God, a belief in a divine government of the world, a distinetion between good and evil, and a hope of a better life, break forth in the *Ṛig-veda*. But the earlier portions of the *Ṛik* allude very little to a future state; and even references to a future state of punishment in all the Vedas are few and far between; and again those references are very obscure. Our ancestors had not contempt for all things beneath the sun, nor had they any dislike for this existence with all its vicissitudes and miseries. So they longed for continuation of life, and death by no other cause than by old age; and also thought of this life simply as a preparation for a new existence in the world of the departed where to enjoy eternal bliss. They however had no idea of retribution after death; and it was their simple faith that the new existence would be merely a continuation of the old age though under changed conditions. There also appears a simple faith that the life in this world is not the last of man;

but after death he is to go to a place of happiness above.* In a passage we read that the highest object of life is to restore that bond which links self to the eternal Self.† There also occurs another passage about being and non-being ; which clearly shows that, that philosophical dogma was known to the Indo-Aryans at so early a period.‡

In the ninth and tenth *mandalas* of the *Rig*-veda there are some distinct references made to a future life. Besides these there are other texts which intimate the same belief. The consciousness of sin is the prominent characteristic of the religion of the Veda. It is said that the gods take away from man the burden of his sins.§ The idea of faith is also found in the *Rig*-veda ;‖ and that faith is again associated sometimes with true scepticism.¶ In the Veda there are to be found certain passages in which

* Prof. Roth, after extracting several passages from the *Rik* in which a belief in immortality is clearly conveyed, says with great force,—"We here find, not without astonishment, beautiful conceptions on immortality, expressed in unadorned language with child-like conviction. If it were necessary, we might here find the most powerful weapons against the view which has lately been revived, and proclaimed as new, that Persia was the only birthplace of the idea of immortality, and that even the nations of Europe had derived it from that quarter ; as if the religious spirit of every gifted race was not able to arrive at it by its own strength."—Journal of the German Oriental Society, iv. p. 427 ; Muir's Original Sanskrit Texts, v. p. 301.

† *Rig*-veda, x. 129, 4.

‡ Taittirîya-Brâhmana, ii, p. 923 : नासदासीन्नो सदासीत् तदानीम् ।

§ *Rig*-veda, i. 162, 22 ; ii. 27, 4 ; iv. 12, 4 ; v. 82, 6 ; vii, 87, 7 ; vi, 93, 7 ; viii. 48, 9 ; x, 25, 3,

‖ Ibid, i. 102, 2 ; i. 104, 6 ; i. 55, 5.

¶ Ibid, viii. 100, 3.

occurs not only the idea of immortality of the soul, of personal immortality, but also of personal responsibility after death. That immortality was gained by a son is mentioned in one passage of the Veda ;* and one poet prays that he may again see his father and mother after death.† It is also said that immortality is secured even by a son.‡ The gods are said to have established the eternal laws of right and wrong ; and they punish sin and reward virtue. Morality and religion were closely connected. But still the enjoyments of a future life are most probably to be understood as of a sensual kind.§ The gods themselves were regarded as subject to the influence of carnal appetites.‖ Some of the hymns attribute to the gods sentiments and passions, such as anger, revenge, and delight in sacrifices ; and represent man with all the desires and weaknesses of his nature. Immunity from taxation is held out as the greatest boon to be received in the next world.¶ A funeral hymn offered to Agni** contains some verses which fully give the views of the writer on a future life. The *pitris*, or fathers of families, who have departed this life and passed to a state of blessedness are represented as objects of adoration to their descendants. The fathers are supplicated almost like gods ; worship

* *Rig*-veda, vii, 56, 24.

† *Rig*-veda, i. 24, 1 ; compare Atharva-veda, xii. 3, 17.

‡ *Rig*-veda, vii. 56, 24 ; compare Gopatha-Brâhmana, i. 1, 2.

§ *Rig*-veda, ix. 113, 7 ff. ; compare Atharva-veda, iv. 34, 2.

‖ *Rig*-veda, iii. 53, 6 ; Atharva-veda, xiv. 2, 31 f.

¶ Atharva-veda, iii. 29, 3.

** *Rig*-veda, x. 16.

and oblations are offered to them ;* and they are said to enjoy in the company of the gods, a life of eternal felicity.† It is said, that there exist three heavens‡ of which the *pitris* occupy the highest. The Vaidik doctrine of the *pitris* chimes in with the Greek and Roman doctrine about the manes. In certain passages of the *R*ig-veda the word *manas* is found to be used for the soul or the animating principle which is never annihilated after the termination of earthly existence.§ *A'tman* is also employed in several portions of the *R*ig-veda for the living principle ; and in some places the sun is also addressed as the soul of all things changeable or unchangeable.‖ Some texts refer indistinctly to the punishment of the wicked.¶ In the Atharva-veda the adjective form of the usual word for hell (*nâraka loka*) occurs : and that region is described as the future abode of the illiberal.**

From the *R*ig-veda we learn that the *R*ishis had conceived the idea of the soul being immortal.†† There is a prayer of Vasish*th*a addressed to Varu*n*a (vii. 86) which

* *R*ig-veda, x. 15, 2, 9 ; see also on the Offerings to the Pitris, Colebrooke's Essay on the Religious Ceremonies of the Hindus.—Miscellaneous Essays, i. pp. 180, ff.

† *R*ig-veda, x. 15, 1 ; Atharva-veda, xviii. 2, 49.

‡ Atharva-veda, xviii. 2, 48.

§ *R*ig-veda, x. 58, 1. Compare Atharva-veda, xviii. 2, 23:–"Let thy soul (*manas*) go to its own and hasten to the fathers." The mind (*manas*) is regarded by the Hindu philosophers as distinct from the soul.

‖ *R*ig-veda, i. 115, 1 ; ix. 2, 10 ; ix. 6, 8 ; ix. 85, 3.

¶ *R*ig-veda, iv. 5, 5 ; vii. 104, 3, ; ix. 73, 8.

** xii. 4, 36.

†† *R*ig-veda, i. 22.

clearly shows the indestructibility of the spirit. There are also some passages which refer to the souls of deceased ancestors as still existing in another world.* It is scarcely to be expected that in such primitive times they would have very clear ideas on this subject; but it is after all worthy to be noticed that long before Greece and Rome became cultivated communities, when Europe was the home of uncivilized barbarians, the *R*ishis had some conception of this doctrine. Modern psychologists cannot teach us more than what was taught by our ancestors some thousand years ago. In the Brâhma*n*as immortality is promised to those who rightly understand and regularly practise the rites of sacrifice. Those who are deficient in this respect and who depart to the next world before the expiration of the natural term of life, are weighed there in a balance.† The doctrine of the Brâhma*n*as is that after death all are born again in the next world, where they are recompensed according to their deeds; the good being rewarded, and the wicked punished.‡ But elsewhere heaven is said to belong only to the Brahmans.§

There are very few passages in the Brâhma*n*as which proclaim the idea of absorption in the deity such as we find in the Upanishads. But from a passage in the *S*atapatha-Brâhma*n*a we learn how in the next world the animals and plants devour men who make a repast of them in this state of existence; unless they are resusciated to life

* *R*ig-veda, i. 36, 18, ; iii. 55, 2 ; vi. 52, 4.

† *S*atapatha-Brâhma*n*a, xi. 2, 7, 33. Compare Proverbs, xvi, 2.

‡ Ibid, vi. 2, 2, 27 ; x. 6, 3, 1 ; xi. 7, 2, 23.

§ Atharva-veda, x. 8, 1.

by the performance of usual ceremonies and sacrifices.*
The word *prâyaschitta* by which expiation or atonement is implied, does not occur in the songs of the *Rig*-veda. But it occurs often in the Brâhma*n*as and the Sûtras in the sense of a means for removing a grievance, or averting an evil; and not in the sense of an atonement for a sin committed.

In the *Rig*-veda Yama is nowhere described in the same manner as in the later mythology.† He is not represented there as a terrible being, but as the ruler of the dead, possessing a beneficient character. He is said to grant to the departed souls a resting place where they may enjoy eternal happiness.‡ Still he is to a certain extent an object of terror and horror. And in a passage of the Atharvan death is said to be his messenger, who conveys the spirits of men to the abode of their forefathers.§ He is also said to have two insatiable dogs with four eyes and wide nostrils, which guard the road to his abode;‖ and he is asked to protect the departed from them.¶ The body which the soul is to take again in the next world, cannot be the one which has undergone cremation, or has been buried in the earth; it may not even be one similar to it, because he is to live henceforth in the company of divine spirits, and so

* xi. 6, 1, 1 ff.

† Wilson's Vishnu-Purâna, p. 216 of Dr. Hall's ed. vol. ii.

‡ Whitney's Oriental and Linguistic Studies, p. 45.

§ xviii. 2, 27.

‖ *Rig*-veda, x. 14, 10-12.

¶ *Rig*-veda, x. 14, 11.

must have such a body as to have a right of place among them.* It is said that the deceased will take his new body, a shining and all glorious spiritual body.† Nowhere in the *R*ig-veda is any trace discoverable of metempsychosis ;‡ which was, no doubt, gradually developed in India itself, but never was it introduced from any foreign country.§ But, on the contrary, it is promised, as the highest reward, that the pious shall again be born in the next world with his earthly body.‖ In certain passages a hope is also held out that the family relations will be maintained in the next world.¶

How the primitive religion and worship of the Indo-Aryans gradually changed and became more and more elaborate and complicated, may be best known from the Vadas themselves. In a history of the ancient Sanskrit literature the Chhandas period is the most interesting and most important in a philosophical point of view. In the Chhandas period, the state of society being simple, religious worship was necessarily so. Now the *R*ishis were

* Roth's article on the Morality of the Vedas in the Journal of the American Oriental Society, iii. p. 343. This paper is, in many respects, very interesting. But there is a ludicrous inconsistency staring us in the face. Poor Yama is charged with the attempt to seduce his sister. The fact as the *R*ig-veda gives it was the reverse. The *sister* longed for cohabitation with her brother, and arguing for his consent to her wishes. Strange, that Dr. Roth did not correct it.

† *R*ig-veda, x. 14, 8.

‡ Wilson's *R*ig-veda, iii. p. xiii. Müller's Chips, i. p. 45.

§ Benfey's Orient und Occident, iii. p. 169. f.

‖ *S*atapatha-Brâhmana, iv. 6, 1, 1 ; xi. 1, 8, 6 ; xii. 8, 3, 31.

¶ Atharva-veda, xii, 3, 17 ; vi. 120, 3.

the priests of their own families to which they imparted religious instructions ; and for which they conducted the daily worship. But in the process of time such a religious worship underwent a gradual but marked change. And as soon as we step into the Mantra and the Brâhma*n*a periods, we observe the gross superstitious character which that primitive religion and worship gradually assumed. In those periods a priesthood was systematically created ; and nothing could be done without a priest.

A'*s*valâyana says that there were four chief priests ; each having three subordinate priests under him.* And these sixteen officiating priests are commonly called by the general term of *Ritvij*.† There were also a compliment of assistants of these sixteen priests, who of course did not rank as *Ritvij*. The Kaushîtakins alone admit the so-called Sadasyas into the *Ritvij*, whose sole business was to superintend all the sacrifices. The priests had peculiar duties to perform, which are prescribed in the Brâhma*n*as. The Adhvaryus had to recite the verses of the Yajur-veda, to measure the ground, to build the *vedi*, or altar, to make the sacrificial vessels, to fetch wood and water, to light the fire, to bring the animal and immolate it. And certainly they constituted the lowest class of priests. The Udgât*r*is had to chant the songs of the Sâma-veda, and to act as the chorus. The peculiar duty of the Hot*r*is was to recite in a distinct and loud voice certain

* *Srauta-sûtras*, iv. 1. See also Kâtyâyana's *Srauta-sûtras*, vii. 1, 6.

† Roth's Sanskrit and German Dictionary *sub voce* ritvij where the appellations of the sixteen kinds of priests are given. See also the passage in the *Satapatha-Brâhmana*, xii. 2 et. seq., there referred to.

verses of the *Rig*-veda in praise of the deities during the time of sacrifices. The Hotris were no doubt, by far the most highly educated class of priests. The Brahmâ had to watch over these three classes of priests, and to remedy any defect which might affect the efficacy of the sacrifice. And the *Rig*-veda itself in one of its latest portions, recognises the superiority of the Brahmâ priest. He was supposed to know the whole ceremonial, and all the three Vedas used by the Hotris, Adhvaryus, and Udgâtris.* The office of a Brahmâ priest was not however a birth right; but every priest could obtain it by assiduous and unremitting study, great ability, and superior ingenuity. The most ancient name of a professional priest was Purohita; and he was more than a chaplain. He was the counsellor of a chief, and the minister of a king, and his companion, too, in peace and war. However, the original institution of a Purohita must not be accepted as a sign of a far advanced hierarchical system. But his office was undoubtedly regarded as a divine institution. Vasishtha and Visvâmitra were the Purohitas of king Sudâsa.† The chief occupation of the

* Müller's History of Ancient Sanskrit Literature, p. 469 ff.

† Visvâmitra, says Signor de Gubernatis (in the Rivista Orientale, i. pp. 409ff., 478ff.), is to be understood as one of the appellations of the sun; and as both the person who holds the name, and Indra are the sons of Kusika, they must be brothers. Vasishtha is the greatest of the Vasus, and means Agni, the solar fire, and points out, like Visvâmitra, to the sun. Sudâsa signifies the horse of the sun, or the sun himself. Ancient Indian tradition speaks of both Visvâmitra and Vasishtha as real historical personages. His theory, therefore, is quite untenable.

Purohita was simply to perform the ordinary sacrifices; but his office even partook of a political character. The ancient appellations of the theologians of the *R*ik as Bahv*r*ichas, those of the Sâman as Chhandogas, and of the Yajus as Adhvaryus are to be found in the Sa*m*hitâ of the Black Yajus and in the *S*atapatha-Brâhma*n*a. The Black Yajus applies the term Adhvaryus to its own adherents, whilst their opponents are called Charakâ-dhvaryus. This natural hostility is also clearly shown in a passage of the Sa*m*hitâ of the White Yajus.* But this spirit of hostility was not exclusively confined to the different schools of the Yajur-veda ; the followers of the Atharva-veda seem to have betrayed similar sectarian jealousies towards the adherents of the other Vedas.†

The term Brahman originally denoted devout worshippers and contemplative sages or poets, who composed hymns in praise of the gods. But after the ceremonial of worship became highly developed and complicated, and the sacred functions became quite distinct from other occupations, the epithet gradually came to be employed for a minister of religion, and at last it came to signify one particular class of priests with certain special duties. Then the hierarchy of the Brahmans was completely organised. Though now priesthood formed an exclusive caste, which for the most part beeame an hereditary order; yet those among other classes that aspired to sacerdotal

* Weber's History of Indian Literature, p. 87 ; Müller's History of Ancient Sanskrit Literature, p. 350.

† Weber's Indische Studien, i. p. 296.

functions and privileges. were also admitted to the same order. Of course as a class some of them were intelligent, some unintelligent, some thoughtful, and some as mere mechanical instruments at the celebration of ceremonial worship.* However, great benefits are said to have resulted from the employment of priests† as their presence was deemed an essential condition of the efficacy of the ritual acts ; and even the highest efficacy is said to result from their intercession.‡ Liberality to them is also mentioned with approbation.§ A superhuman power was ascribed to the priests ;‖ and curses were fulminated against their oppressors.¶ But the comparison of frogs to them implies a total disregard for them and for their functions.** The sacred and divinely consecrated majesty of the priests was not unfrequently assailed by the ungodly ; and consequently they had to encounter much difficulty to enforce a due regard which they themselves attached to the performance of religious rites. And we thus find a long list of condemnatory epithets applied to those persons who were the deniers of the gods, and who were averse to the rites. The Kalpa works enjoin that the Hotri is to perform his duties with the *Rik*, the

* *Rig-veda*, viii. 50, 9.

† Atharva-veda, iii. 19.

‡ *Rig-veda*, vii. 83, 4.

§ *Rig-veda*, i. 125 ; i. 126 ; v. 27 ; v. 30, 12 ff ; v. 61, 10 ; vi. 27, 8 ; vi, 47 ; 22 ff.

‖ Atharva-veda, xix. 9, 12 ; xix. 43, 8.

¶ Atharva-veda, xii. 5.

** *Rig-veda*, vii. 103.

Udgâtri with the Sâman, the Adhvaryu with the Yajus, and the Brahmâ with all the three Vedas.

Religion is nothing without a worship and without a cultus ; and, in fact, the origin and growth of sacrifice is an important page in the history of the human mind. The chapter on sacrifices may be dull, monotonous and uninteresting ; but by a critical examination of them we are enabled to determine step by step the different stages of civilization, through which the eastern branch of the whole Aryan family passed. Some sacrifices, no doubt, belong to the pastoral stage of civilization, some to the agricultural stage of civilization, and some attest to the chivalrous character of the times. The Smârta-sacrifices were such as properly belonged to the pastoral and agricultural stages of civilization. But the *S*rauta-sacrifices could be performed only by a prosperous community at once chivalrous and enterprising. The Soma-sacrifice belonged to the period of chivalry ; and the *R*ig-veda also abounds in passages which at once exhibit the chivalrous character of the times. The system of Vaidik sacrifices throws an immense light on many a dark point in the history of the Indo-Aryans ; and there is no doubt that the sacrifices, upon the whole, exercised a most potent influence upon their social and religious polity. Sacrifices were not all for the first time instituted in India ; but a good many were brought from their cradle in central Asia where they must have passed through those stages before emigration took place. In India certainly those rites and ceremonies again underwent radical and most extensive changes. In the earlier part of the Vaidik times the first duty which the Indo-Aryans owed to their gods, was the performance of their worship with its ceremonies; and that form of worship, no doubt, was simple, patriarchal and domestic. It was performed three times daily simply with hymns and prayers very often accompanied with fruits and the products of the flocks which were offered on the family altars. This established order of worship with its ceremonies is called *rita*. The ceremonial worship was not left to the charge of the priests; it was but a spontaneous act of devotion, and was neither tedious nor complicated in its minor details. But when in the course of time the priests formed themselves into a privileged class worship and ceremonies underwent immense modifications. And thus most of the rites gradually required the sacrifice of a large number of various kinds of beasts and birds. The rites, offerings, oblations and sacrifices were all performed with the distinct purpose either to avert an evil or to secure a coveted object by divine intercession, or to propitiate the gods themselves. They were offered to gain the good will of some offended deity, or through the dread of others.

At the celebration of the Darsapûrnamâsa sacrifices the Adhvaryus had to place the cows and calves together, and to touch the calves with the branch of a tree. This sacrifice was celebrated at new and full moon. Besides this, we have innumerable names of sacrifices; of which the Râjasuya, Agnihotra, Asvamedha, Somayâga and Purushamedha are by far the most remarkable. The Asvamedha or horse-sacrifice was probably adopted by the Indians from the Scythians, before they crossed the Indus.* At this sacrifice 609 animals of various descriptions, domestic and wild, were tied to 21 posts, but after the customary prayers had been offered up, they were three times led round the sacrificial fire. Elephants, camels,† buffaloes, birds, porpoises, crocodiles, snakes, and even mosquitoes and worms were included among the animals. At last the horse was immolated by an axe, and its flesh was cut up into fragments, dressed, partly roasted, and partly boiled, and made into balls and eaten. This ceremony was subsequently performed symbolically.‡ The sacrifice of the horse, and that of the cow, no doubt, were common in the earliest periods of the Vaidik ritual. The Brâhma*n*a of the Black Yajus and both the Kalpa and the G*ri*hya-sûtras distinctly mention the different occasions when cattle should be slaughtered and eaten. It is no less a fact that the meat of cattle was required for the due celebration of scores of other ceremonies ; and more particularly the Râjasuya, the Vâjapeya, the A*s*vamedha, the Pancha*s*âradîya sava, and the Sûla gava could not have been performed without it. The proper place for the performance of the Sûla gava rite was outside a village or a town, unfrequented by men, and the time was after midnight. The Gomedha was not certainly typical as many are disposed to believe. The Gavâmanayana was held for four days. It formed a part of the Mahâ-

* Herodotus, iv. 71.

† Compare Sanskrit *kramela* and Greek *kamēlos.*

‡ Wilson's Introduction to the *Rig-veda.*

plava, Dvâdasâha, and a few other ceremonies; but it did not constitute a distinct rite by itself. The Sarvamedha or All-sacrifice and the Brahmayajna are passed over in the *S*atapatha-Brâhma*n*a. They find place in the A'ra*n*yaka of the Taittirîyas, but not in their Brâhma*n*a. The Pit*r*imedha or Sacrifice to the Manes has place in the A'ra*n*yaka as well as in the Brâhma*n*a of the Taittirîyas. The Purushamedha or Man-sacrifice required the actual sacrifice of man; and it had for its distinct object the acquisition of independent sovereignty over all created beings. But in reality it was entirely of an expiatory nature. It required full forty days for its celebration; and a hundred and eighty-five men of various tribes, characters, and professions were essentially required to be bound to eleven posts and consecrated to various deities. The holocausts of human victims formed part of the ancient cultus of India; and there is a strong presumptive evidence that *S*una*h*sepa was intended for an actual immolation. It is beyond doubt that the Indo-Aryans were familiar with the idea of human sacrifice.* It also found favor with the Druids, the Scythians, and the Phœnicians; and some traces of it are found even in the Bible. The earliest indication of the rite occurs in the *R*ig-veda, in the Vâjasaneyi-Sa*m*hitâ of the White Yajur-veda and the *S*atapatha-Brâhma*n*a. The Aitareya and the Taittirîya-Brâhma*n*as also refer to it.

* Wilson's Essay on Human Sacrifice in the Veda; Roth, in Weber's Indische Studien, i. pp. 457-464; and ii. pp. 111-123; Weber's History of Indian Literature, p. 84.

The principal object for which the Sâma-veda was composed, was the performance of those sacrifices in which the juice of the Soma plant was principally required. And of such sacrifices the most remarkable is the Jyotish*t*oma, which consists of seven stages; but the celebration of the first stage or the Agnish*t*oma alone was deemed obligatory, while the other six stages, such as the Atyagnish*t*oma, Ukthya, Sho*d*a*s*in, Atirâtra, Aptoryâma, and Vâjapeya, though adding to the virtue of the sacrificer, were considered as voluntary. The Soma was from the earliest times connected with the religious history of the Indo-Aryans;* and was thus elevated to the proud position of a god. The *R*ig-veda is replete with its praises; and the other three Vedas also contain *mantras* to be recited at all the stages of its manufacture. The high antiquity of this cultus is attested by the references to it to be found in the Zand-Avesta.† The plants were gathered by the roots on the hills on a moonlight night, and after being stripped of their leaves they were brought in carts drawn by two rams or he-goats to the house of the sacrificer. The stalks then were deposited in the hall of oblation, and bruised and crushed between stones, and placed with the juice in a sieve of goats' hair, and were further pressed

* Windischmann's Dissertation on the Soma worship of the Arians; Whitney's Main Results of the Later Vaidik Researches in Germany; Lassen's Indian Antiquities, i. p. 516; and Roth's articles in the Journal of the German Oriental Society, for 1848 (pp. 216ff.) and 1850 (pp. 417 ff.)

† Plutarch de Isid. et Osir. 46, in which the Soma, or as it is in Zand, *haoma*, appears to be referred to under the appellation of *omomi*.

and squeezed by the priests' ten fingers one or two of which being ornamented by rings of flattened gold. Finally, the juice mixed with barley, wheat, and clarified butter was allowed to ferment; and was then drawn off in a scoop called *sruch*, and offered up thrice daily to the gods, and a ladleful was taken by the priests. From the Vaidik descriptions of the effects of the Soma nectar on the gods, to whom it was the most acceptable and delightful oblation, we are to believe that it was a fermented intoxicating beverage; and this again we can assume from our knowledge of the effects produced by its use in men. The expressed juice of the Soma creeper itself had not either its narcotic property or its keeping quality; but it being diluted with water, mixed with clarified butter, barley meal, and the meal of wild paddy or *nivâra*, and at last being left to ferment in a jar for nine days, it acquired its exhilarating and inebriating effects.* While it was invested with a sacramental and religious character, it was by no means manufactured for sale. But it was in all cases preserved in a bag of cowskin.†

* Stevenson's Sâma-veda, p. iii-vi; Haug's Aitareya-Brâhmana, i. p. 6; Manning's Ancient India, i. p. 86.

† *Rig*-veda, v. 5, 19.

CHAPTER III.

General Character of the Vedas—the Vaidik Dialect—and the Chronology of the Vaidik Age.

SIR WILLIAM JONES said that the student of Indo-Aryan literature and religion found himself in the presence of infinity. As Homer was the sole repository of intellectual culture in Greece, so the Vedas are here in India. The original texts of the four Vedas, and the immense body of literary records which had grouped themselves about them by gradual accretion, form a bulk so incredibly vast and of such enormous importance that not the whole body of sacred literature of any one ancient nation can be compared with that of the Indo-Aryans. Whatever was handed down, as a sacred trust, from father to son, soon received a kind of hallowed character; and also derived its importance from the circumstance to which its origin was due. Our Aryan fathers handed to us the scriptural Vedas, which have been canonized as time wore on; and which, notwithstanding many puerilities and repulsive legends, arrest our thoughts and inspire us with keen interest. They looked upon their venerated scriptures as the foundation of their power and prestige. Our heart grows warm when we find the Vedas to be strewn with original and at the same time sober and profound ideas, pure and sublime conceptions, and lofty sentiments which were by no means unworthy of our most distant ancestors. In them we read at any rate the reflex of the laws and thoughts of a divine being; and they seem to contain the thread which links the present with the past. To the Vedas must be attached an undying interest and an ever increasing value not only for their greatest antiquity, but also for the immense flood of light which they throw on the primitive state of the Indo-Aryan society, Indo-Aryan speech, and general mythology. We do not yet find in them any traces of a growing religion or a growing language; nevertheless we gain from them a real insight into the feelings, the aspirations, the thoughts, the fears, the hopes, the doubts, and the faith of our ancestors. And in process of time the Vaidik religion, whatever it was, has become, through the corruptions and prejudices, of a most revolting type, of successive ages, a heterogenous medley of theology, philosophy and science.

Beyond doubt, India with her ancient and illustrious name hoary with hallowed traditions, claims a very high antiquity as well as a distinguished rank among the civilized countries of the ancient world. But unfortunately, there is nothing historical in Sanskrit literature which records the heroic exploits of the Indo-Aryans;* and the word *history* itself is unknown in their language. Indeed, the Indo-Aryans never possessed any true historical

* Burnouf's History of Indian Buddhism, p. iii.

sense.' However, to get an insight into the state of the civilization of the Vaidik age, it is necessary that we should refer to the pages of the Vedas* themselves. The Vedas are the ancient *S*âstra of the Indo-Aryans, or, as now they are called, the Hindûs.† The Vedas are far

* The word Veda is derived from the Sanskrit root *vid*, to know, and is the same with the Greek *id-*, Latin *vid-*, Gothic *vait-*; and may be translated into *knowing* or *knowledge*.

† It is interesting to inquire into the origin of the term *Hindû*. It occurs with the whole treasure of Sanskrit words in the *S*abda-kalpa-Druma, and therefore it may seem to many that it is of Sanskrit origin. But the authority which has been cited in it from the Merutantra, xxiii, to prove that it is such, shows, on the contrary, that it is a modern word. In fact, the Tantras are wanting in the halo of antiquity. The oldest among them, says Dr. Râjendralâla Mitra, was not composed before the 3rd century of Christ, and the majority of them probably between the 6th and the 12th century. There is, however, a word equivalent to the national name in the Zand. And it also re-appears as Hoddû for Hondû in a portion of the Hebrew scriptures called Esther. The term Hindû is not found to appear in any of the ancient Sanskrit authors. Indeed, this word was never employed in the Sanskrit language. But nevertheless it is not of very modern origin. Herodotus (iv. 44; v. 3) has noticed the Hindûs under the general appellation of *Indoi*. The word Hindû was derived from Sindhu; and the ancient Persians must have at first used that term, as it is established and it cannot be gainsaid, that according to Zand grammar the term Hindû owes its origin to Sindhu or Hindhu as pronounced by them. In the Vendîdâd (i. 73) we have the expression Hapta-Hendu which is nothing more than a transformation of the Sanskrit Sapta-Sindhavas, the land of the seven rivers, which was a designation of the Vaidik India. It was also very well known to the Romans in the days of Augustus (Virgil's Eneid, ix. 30). In the Cuneiform Inscriptions Hidus is used for Sapta-Sindhavas, and it should be so understood.—See Spiegel's Avesta, i. p. 66, note 3.

unlike the Qur'ân as "an endless incoherent rhapsody of fable and precept, and declaration, which seldom excites a sentiment or an idea, which sometimes crawls in the dusts and is sometimes lost in the clouds."* That our ancestors looked on the Vedas with the greatest possible reverence is no marvel. The Vedas were, no doubt, their first national efforts in the department of literature. In them we catch astronomical observations in their primary stage, philosophical thoughts in their first dawn, mythology in the course of formation, poetry gradually rising to unmistakeable excellence; and even the first attempts in the department of grammar and glossary. And they reflect the growth and development of the national life of the Aryan world. It is our belief that no service more important could be rendered to the history of our race, than to diffuse the knowledge and encourage the investigation of the Vaidik writings.

The Vedas which stand at the head of the whole body of Indian literature, are altogether a peculiar class of writings. They are each, upon the whole, composed of the same identical matter; they also harmonize with one another in external form and language, and even in the nature of their contents. But when we take into consideration such other matters as are their peculiar characteristics, internal arrangement, the date, and object of collection, and their use at the worship of the various gods, or at some of the ceremonials having close relation with various grand events in the domestic or public life of the

* Gibbon's Roman Empire, i. p. 269.

Indo-Aryans, they appear respectively to be of an altogether dissimilar character.

The word Veda is significantly employed to designate those ancient Sanskrit works, in which is laid the foundation of Brahmanic belief; and these works were originally three, i. e., the *R*ig-veda, the Sâma-veda, and the Yajur-veda. The frequent mention of the Indian scriptures is made in ancient Sanskrit literature under the name of *traî-vidyâ*, or the triple science.* The Veda is and remains three-fold; and the triple Veda is comprehended under the name of *mantra*. But at a more subsequent period a fourth Veda was added to them; though it was never held as sacred as its predecessors were. However, they are now commonly four in number, viz., the *R*ig-veda—Veda of hymns, the Sâma-veda—Veda of chants, the Yajur-veda—Veda of sacrificial formulas, and the Atharva-veda—Veda of incantations. Manu, in his Institutes, often speaks of the three first Vedas calling them *trayam brahma sanâtanam*;† and he mentions only once (xi. 33) "the revelations of the Atharvângirasas" alluding to, but not designating by name, the Atharva-veda. Amara Simha, in his Kosha, also notices only three Vedas;‡ but refuses the Atharvan a place among them. The Atharva-veda is not mentioned in the Chhândogya-upanishad (iv. 17, 1); and the Kaushîtaki-Brâhmana also omits to mention it.§ But in the Atharva-

* Satapatha-Brâhmana, iv. 6, 7, 1; Aitareya-Brâhmana, v. 32.

† Manu i. 23.

‡ स्त्रियां ऋक् साम यजुषी इति वेदास्त्रयस्त्रयी ।

§ Müller's History of Ancient Sanskrit Literature, p, 457.

veda itself it is reckoned among the Vedas under the designation of the Atharvans and Angirases (x. 7, 20); and it is similarly alluded to in the *S*atapatha-Brâhma*n*a (xiii. 4, 3, 7). And in the ninth verse of the Purusha-sûkta it is even mentioned and designated under the title of Chhandas. "The true reason why the three first Vedas are often mentioned without any notice of the fourth, must be sought, not in their different origin and antiquity, but in the difference of their use and purport."*

The *R*ig-veda is extant only in the recension of the *S*âk-alas; and we have only references to the other recension of the Vâshkalas. But the difference between the two was not very considerable; the Vâshkalas had only eight hymns more. Although the greater portion of the hymns of the *R*ik-Sa*m*hitâ was composed on the banks of the Indus; their final redaction certainly took place in India proper during the period when the Brahmanical element had become predominant; and the Kosala-Videhas and the Kuru-Panchâlas had the chief merit of having effected it.† The *R*ik is to the student of history the Veda *par excellence.* The *R*ig-veda is no less a repository of the hymns which were composed after our early ancestors had reached the land of their adoption, and with which they addressed the gods in whom they believed, and extolled other matters with a spontaneous freshness and simplicity, than it is a store-house of also those hymns which they had brought with them as the most precious heirloom from their

* Colebrooke's Essays, i. p. 13.

† Weber's History of Indian Literature, pp. 10 ff.

ancient home to the West.* The hymns which they brought with them were preserved in families as single and unconnected compositions for several centuries solely by tradition, and thus they must have undergone an amount of wear and tear; and Prof. Aufrecht very justly remarks that possibly only a small portion of such hymns may have been preserved to us in the *R*ik.† The *R*ig-veda consists, with a few exceptions, of detached prayers dedicated to divinities now no longer worshipped, some of whom are even entirely unknown. And in point of time and even literary development it is the oldest of books and the earliest depository of Aryan faith. The Yajus, the Sâman, and the Atharvan presuppose the *R*ik; and the anteriority of the *R*ik to the Brâhma*n*as is proved not only by the frequent allusions which are made to the former by the latter, but also by the words and phrases employed in the hymns themselves. The language and style of the *R*ik is artificial, and its poetry is utterly deficient in natural sublimity; there is, however, one redeeming feature in it namely that most of the hymns contain moral ideas and spiritual hopes and aspirations. Though there is little that is attractive and beautiful in the *R*ik, and though some of its hymns are utterly insipid and have no life or meaning at all; yet the volume itself gives life to antiquity, and gives us a real and living idea of our early ancestors. As a complete panorama of

* Langlois, Preface to his French translation of the *R*ig-veda, i. pp. x. xi. See also Journal of the American Oriental Society, iv. p. 249.

† Weber's Indische Studien, iv. p. 8.

ancient religion it reveals to us the very beginnings of human life and thought. Fortunately, there is no system in the *Rik*.

The *Rik*-Sa*m*hitâ is a lyrical collection; and those lyrics are of the simplest form. We hardly find in it high flights of poetical fancy; and there is least trace of abstraction. There is no doubt that it was composed in the infancy of the human race. As a real stratum of ancient thought and religion, the *Rik* contains many things which are now quite unintelligible to us. The *Rik* however contains some really historical elements; and Prof. Roth very justly calls it the historical Veda. The *Rik* is evidently composed of heterogeneous materials. Its first seven books bear a similar character, arranged upon a like plan. These books embrace the oldest, the most genuine and the most sacred hymns; and retain, as far as the tradition goes, an integral and not incongruous whole; and palpably remain as it was originally fixed and arranged. The eighth and ninth books present quite a different system of internal arrangement. The tenth book corresponds with the arrangement of two of its predecessors, and copiously supplies us with the most distinct evidences of a later origin. In various instances, the tradition is very unreliable with reference to the authorship of the hymns, and even in certain cases it is found to attribute some of them to mythical personages.

The hymns now united into a Sa*m*hitâ, had existed in detached forms, and were preserved as sacred heirlooms in different families, before they were aggregated together and arranged in the order in which we now find them. The hymns are arranged in the order of the deities addressed, and in accordance with the families of various *r*ishis which are credited with their authorship. And this classification is no doubt based upon a scientific principle. It is very probable, that the redaction of the text may have taken place at a later date than those of the Sâman and of the Yajus. The first eight books comprise hymns which are addressed to Agni, Indra, the Vi*s*ve-devâ*h* and other divinities. The ninth is solely dedicated to Soma, which has the closest connexion with the Sâman; whereas the tenth mainly supplied the materials for the Atharva-veda. The same hymn which is dedicated to the same deity, is, however, sometimes addressed to different divinities. Many hymns also partake of the nature of petitions or panegyrics addressed to eminent chiefs or heroes either living or dead. But the general form of the hymns is dialogistic. The hymns are to be understood as combining the attributes of both prayer and praise; and in them the goodness, the generosity, the power, the vastness, and even the personal beauty of the deities are described with no end of rhetorical flourish. And also those deities are besought to confer blessings which are for the most part of a worldly and physical character; as food, wealth, a long life, a large family, power, cattle, cows, horses, protection against enemies, complete victory over them, and sometimes their utter destruction.* But the hymns themselves afford no directions for their employment, and make no mention of the

* Wilson's *R*ig-veda, i. p. xxiii ff.; Roth's Literature and History of the Veda, p. 8.

occasions on which they are to be applied, or of the ceremonies at which they are to be chanted.*

A large number of hymns of the *R*ik-Sa*m*hitâ are repeated in the other Vedas; while none of the verses which properly belong to the latter are to be met with in the former. The collection of the *richas* in a systematic form should be attributed rather to more scientific causes. And we may even suppose that science in this case may have overdone her work; and instead of subjecting the hymns to a considerable modification, may have also improved upon them, and so transmitted to us a *rifacimento*.

We find in the *R*ik-Sa*m*hitâ a few hymns known by the name of *Khilas*, which were added at the end of each chapter after the whole collection of the ten books had been completed. The *Khilas*, as the Vaidik apocrypha, must be looked upon as a link closely connecting the Vaidik hymns with the latter parts of the Indo-Aryan literature. We are only to accept them as successful imitations of the real and genuine songs; but as such they acquired a certain degree of sanctity and dignity. They also gradually crept into the Sa*m*hitâs of the other Vedas; they are even referred to in the Brâhma*n*as, although they are not counted in the Anukrama*n*îs. There is also another class of hymns called *dânastutis* or praises of certain kings for their gifts to the priests.† These hymns wear, upon the whole, a modern character; and they may be assigned to the latter part of the Mantra period.

* Wilson's *R*ig-veda, i. p. viii. † Colebrooke's Essays, i. p. 22.

The *R*ik-Sam*h*itâ is certainly a wonderful work; and proves that the Indo-Aryan mind had been scientifically developed long before the age of the poems of Homer or Hesiod. It must not be assumed that the hymns of this Veda are purely of a religious character. A hymn in the seventh book recounts in a singularly jocular manner the revival of the frogs at the commencement of the rains, and likens their croaking to the singing of the Brahmans in ceremonial worships.* It is certainly a curious fact that the same animal was selected by the earliest satirist of Greece as the representative of the Homeric heroes.† Again, in the tenth book we have the lamentation of a gamester over his ruinous devotion to play.‡ Numerous other instances of a similar nature might be easily adduced. In all probability those portions, which are considered as non-religious, belong to a later period.

The hymns of the *R*ik themselves are apparently of different periods spreading over several centuries; some among them being older and some more recent.§ When we read of any *R*ishi speaking of his own hymn as new, we must conclude that he was of course acquainted with

* *Rig*-veda, vii. 103.

† Müller's Ancient Sanskrit Literature, pp. 494 f.

‡ *Rig*-veda, x. 34.

§ i. 12, 11; i. 27, 4; i. 60, 3; i. 89, 3; i. 96, 2; i. 130, 10; i. 143, 1; ii. 17, 1; ii. 24, 1; iii. 1, 20; vi. 17, 13; vi. 22, 7; vi. 44, 13; vi. 48, 11; vi. 50, 6. Max Müller designates the most ancient portion of the hymns by the term *Chhandas*, and those that are comparatively modern, *Mantra* (see his History of Ancient Sanskrit Literature, pp. 70, 525 ff). But it is to be observed that he is altogether singular in the use of these two words in the above senses, as they nowhere obtain in the ancient Sanskrit many of the older hymns of the same kind. The relative antiquity of the different hymns can only be determined by their general contents, ideas, language, style and metre.* The old hymns, however, were displaced by the new; but the former were held as sacred as the latter. The authors of the new hymns had to borrow many thoughts and words from the old ones; and such repititions often occur in their compositions.† And the proof of the antiquity of the Vaidik hymns lies in the fact that many words used in the Veda afterwards became obsolete. Then, in fact, the refinements of grammar had no existence. The hymns are drawn up in a great variety of metres, most of which are peculiar to them. The metres so employed show a long and successful cultivation of the rhythmical art

writers. Excepting the Bráhmana portion the rest is generally called *Mantra.* In the Purusha-sûkta (x. 909) even Chhandas is put for the Atharvan; and the Atharvan itself is also referred to under the same designation in one of its own verses (xi. 7, 24). Pâṇini in his grammar repeatedly speaks of the Vedas in the general term of *Chhandas,* though indicating sometimes the Mantra portion, and sometimes even the Bráhmana portion (Goldstücker's Pâṇini, p. 71). In the entire collection of ancient and modern Sanskrit literature, *Chhandas* is applied exclusively to the whole body of the Vedas. But *Chhandas* is nowhere employed for the most ancient portions of the Veda nor *Mantra* for those that are comparatively modern. Müller (Chips, i. p. 84) further considers that *Zand* and *Chhandas* are both equivalent terms; *Zand* being a corruption of the Sanskrit *Chhandas.* Although they seem to resemble in sound and letter, yet there is nothing of affinity in signification. *Zand* is used in the sense of *commentary, explanation,* or *gloss;* while *Chhandas* in the ancient writers means *metre.*

* Muir's Original Sanskrit Texts, iii. p. 224.

† Langlois, *Ṛig*-veda, i. p. xiii.

We meet with the technical names of the metres in the latter portions of the *Rik*. And the entire body of hymns abound also in similes or metaphors distinguished by a vein of naïve observations ; which certainly show a considerable amount of shrewdness and worldly wisdom possessed by the Indo-Aryans. It is, however, beyond doubt that the aggregate assemblage of hymns which comprises the *Rik-Samhitâ*, could never have been composed by the men of one or even two generations ; and it is to be especially observed here in connexion with this point that there are hymns composed by the sons as well as by their fathers and earlier ancestors ;* and this fact is amply borne out by the passages of the hymns themselves which make an apparent distinction between the *Rishis* as ancient and modern. This acknowledgment attests to the existence of the historical element in the Veda. It is, of course, an acknowledgment on the part of the hymnists themselves that numerous persons had existed ; and a series of events occurred long before their own age.† The line which apparently separated the moderns from the ancients was undoubtedly traced by the immigration of the Indo-Aryans into India ; which was regarded by them as the greatest event in their annals, and which marked a new epoch in their chronology. It is most probable that several centuries must have elapsed between the composition of the oldest and that of the most recent *richas* ; and in this intervening period the Indo-Aryan community passed through

* i. 1, 2 ; i. 48, 14 ; i. 118, 3 ; i. 131, 6 ; iv. 50, 1 ; vi. 21, 1 ; vi. 22, 2 ; vii. 53, 1 ; vii. 76, 4 ; ix. 110, 7 ; x. 14, 15.

† Muir's Original Sanskrit Texts, iii. p. 219.

various stages of development, social, moral, religious and intellectual.

The first book of the *R*ik-Sa*m*hitâ contains one hundred and ninety-one hymns which are with some exceptions, ascribed to fifteen different authors such as Gotama, Ka*n*va, Kutsa, *S*una*h*sepa, Kakshîvan, Agastya, &c. The second containing forty-three hymns is attributed to G*r*itsamada; the third, sixty-two, to Vi*s*vâmitra; the fourth, fifty-eight to Vâmadeva; the fifth, eighty-seven, to Atri; the sixth, seventy-five, to Bharadvâja; the seventh, one hundred and four, to Va*s*ish*t*ha; the eighth, which is entitled *pragâthâs*, ninety-two, (besides 11 Vâlkhilya-sûktas) to Ka*n*va; the ninth, one hundred and fourteen, to Angiras; and the tenth, one hundred and ninety-one, to *R*ishis of different families and also to mythical personages. The names of the authors are given here; however by these names we are to understand even their families. The Sûktas or hymns again are distinguished by different names, such as Mahâ-sûkta, Kshudra-sûkta, Madhyam-sûkta, *R*ishi-sûkta, Devatâ-sûkta, and Chhanda*h*-sûkta; and these terms are applied simply to designate a certain scientific arrangement of the entire mass of the *sûktas* specially with reference to the deity, author, metre, and quantity of *richas* of each of them. The worship to which some of the hymns of the *R*ik are devoted, must have been purely of a sacrificial character; and such worship consisted more of detached sacrificial ceremonials than of a series of sacrifices of a complicated character. Yet, there are to be found hymns, which apparently indicate the existence, at the time of their composition, of highly complicated and artificial rituals. But it does not, therefore, follow that the *Rik* as such, was drawn up for the purpose of being chanted at those rituals. The Yajur-veda and the Sâma-veda are indispensable for liturgic purposes; but, such is not the case with the *Rik*. The *Rik* must have preceded the completion of those ritual acts. Though many of the verses of the *Rik* are used at religious rites, yet there remain a good many which have no such purposes; and those verses are purely of a poetical or mystical character. Again, the Yajur-veda and the Sâma-veda are arranged in conformity with the sacrificial acts to which they apply; but the arrangement followed in the *Rik* is altogether different from them, and not with reference to such acts. The *Rik*, therefore, cannot have borne originally a ritual stamp.

The Sâma-veda is an anthology, and purely a derivative production. This Veda was at one time the most comprehensive of the four Vedas. It is more copious than the Yajus and the Atharvan, though not equal to the *Rik*. It is, however, nothing more than a recast of the *Rik*, being composed, with some exceptions, of the very same hymns, which are in their *rich*-form, although with the *sâman*-accents. The Sâman is also remarkably deficient in literary and historical interest. Burnell* and Aufrecht† urge against the superior antiquity of the readings of the Sâman, as compared with those of the *Rik*-Sa*m*hitâ. The Sâma-Sa*m*hitâ has come down to us in two recensions; one of which belongs to the school of the

* A'rsheya-Brâhma*n*a, p. xvi. ff.

† Hymnen des *Rig*-veda, pp. xvi., xvii.

Râ*n*âyanîyas, and the other to that of the Kauthumas. These recensions, upon the whole, differ very little from each other. The Sâman consists of two parts:—the A'rchika or Pûrvârchika, also called Chhandograntha; and Staubhika or Uttarârchika, also called Uttarâgrantha. The A'rchika which is arranged into fifty-nine decades and divided into chapters and half-chapters, is composed of five hundred and eighty-five verses, of which five hundred and thirty-nine are taken from the *R*ik; and as adapted to the general and frequent use of the priests, exists in two forms, called Gânas, the Grâmageya-gâna (erroneously called Veya-gâna) which is divided into seventeen prapâ*t*hakas; and the A'ra*n*ya-gâna into six prapâ*t*hakas. The A'ra*n*ya comprises songs adapted for recitation in forests; and the Veya-gâna embraces such songs as are to be chanted in towns. The Staubhika which is distributed over nine chapters and subdivided into half-chapters, contains twelve hundred and twenty-five verses, of which eleven hundred and ninety-four are appropriated from the *R*ik. This portion exists in the same manner in two forms, called the U'ha-gâna which is divided into twenty-three prapâ*t*hakas; and the U'hya-gâna into six prapâ*t*hakas. The Sâman, however, contains no indication which may determine approximately the period of its origin. This Veda among other Vedas has a peculiar feature of its own in as much as it is provided with a system of accents which consist of no less than ten different signs. The chief object of this collection must have been, as it appears from its special characteristics, that its *richas* should be chanted during the ceremonies of Soma offering and on different other ceremonial occasions. The verses contained in the Sâman are arranged according to their subjects; and the principal metres employed in the whole collection are the Gâyatrî, V*r*ihati, Trishtubh, Anushtubh, Jagati, Sarkari, Kakva, and Pankti. The songs are consecrated to Agni, Indra, Prajâpati, Soma, Varu*n*a, Tvastâ, Angirâ, Pushâ, Sarasvatî and Indrâgni. And the style of the Veda is, upon the whole, very antiquated.

Prof. Benfey has shown in the preface (p. xix.) to his valuable edition of the Sâma-Sa*m*hitâ that there exist in it some verses, the absence of which in the *R*ik is conspicuous. The total absence of seventy-one verses as found in the recensions of the Sâman, from the recension in which we now possess the *R*ik-Sa*m*hitâ, must only be accounted for by the circumstance, that these verses belonged in fact to one or the other of the recensions of the *R*ik, which have now altogether perished.* The relation of the Sâman with the *R*ik is to a certain degree analogous to that between the White and the Black Yajus.† The Sâman and the Yajus are the attendants of the *R*ik.‡ The Sâman cannot be considered as an enlargement of the original Veda; but the case of the Yajus is quite different. Both contain different readings varying in greater or less degree from those of the *R*ig-Veda Sa*m*hitâ. The *richas* occuring in the Sâma-Veda Sa*m*hitâ

* Müller's History of Ancient Sanskrit Literature, p. 475.

† Weber's Indische Studien, i. p. 63 ff.

‡ Kaushîtaki-Brâhma*n*a, vi. 11 : तत्परिचरणावितरौ वेदौ ।

and the Yaju*h*-Sa*m*hitâ are, with some exceptions, borrowed in an altered form from the *R*ik-Sa*m*hitâ ; and those detached *richas* again appear to exhibit very little harmony with the text of the latter. But the *richas* found in the Sâman are to be taken as older and more original on account of the greater antiquity of their grammatical forms than those of the two Sa*m*hitâs of the Yajus where they have undergone a secondary modification.* Some of the Sûtras of the Sâman are little more than lists, such as we find in the Anukrama*n*îs, appended to the Vedas. Their style, upon the whole, very nearly approaches the style of the Sûtra works.

The Yajur-veda is in a double form : the Black Yajus or the Taittirîya-Sa*m*hitâ and the White Yajus or the Vâjasaneyi-Sa*m*hitâ. These, in the main, have the same matter; but they seem to differ from each other only as regards their details and arrangement. In the Black Yajus the formulas for the entire sacrificial ceremonial are generally accompanied by dogmatical explanations, and ritual supplements ; while in the White Yajus the case is quite different. There they form subjects that are entirely distinct from one another. The Black Yajus is the older of the two.† The White embraces texts which are not found in the Black ; and when viewed in reference to the motley character of the latter the former looks 'white,' or orderly. The White is manifestly intended as an improvement on the Black. But these two

* Weber's History of Indian Literature, p. 9.

† Goldstücker's Literary Remains, i. p. 277.

different divisions must have displayed a good deal of antagonism towards each other.* The Black and the White Yajus originated, no doubt, with a schism of which Yâjnavalkya was most probably the author.† They originated in the eastern parts of Hindustan, in the country of the Kurupanchâlas, and they belong to a period when the Brahmanical organisation and the system of caste were completely consolidated.‡ Three different recensions of the Black Yajus are known to us; one that of A'pastamba, a sub-division of the Khâ*nd*ikîyas; the other, the Kâ*t*haka, which belongs to the school of the Charakas; and another the A'treya, a sub-division of the Aukhîyas. The A'pastambîyas belong to southern India, and their founder was a native of A'ndhra country or the districts between the Godâvarî and the Krish*n*â.§ The existence of the A'ndhra kingdom was also known to Pliny.‖ The Sa*m*hitâ of the Black Yajus is in fact a medley of undigested fragments of all sorts. It comprises seven kâ*nd*as or books; these again include forty-four prapâ*t*hakas or chapters, embracing altogether six hundred and fifty-one anuvâkas or sections, which are arranged in two thousand, one hundred and ninety-eight ka*nd*ikâs or portions. The recensions of the White Yajus bear the names of the

* Weber's Indische Studien, i. p. 296.

† Wilson's Works, v. p. 332.

‡ Weber's History of Indian Literature, p. 107.

§ Cunningham's Geography, p. 527 seqq., Burnell's South Indian Palæography, p. 14, note 2.

‖ Pliny, Hist. Nat. vi. 22.

Kâ*n*vas and of the Mâdhya*m*dinas.* The White Yajus in the Mâdhya*m*dina recension is arranged into forty adhyâyas or lectures, divided into three hundred and three anuvâkas or sections, containing one thousand, nine hundred and seventy-five ka*nd*ikâs or portions. The last fifteen adhyâyas of the White Yajus are of considerably later origin ;† and the last adhyâya is also regarded as an Upanishad. And the redaction of the Yajus was accomplished by the Kurupanchâlas and Kosala-Videhas when they were in their prime.‡ The Black Yajus contains the formulas for the entire sacrificial ceremonial, such as those to be found in the Sa*m*hitâ of the White Yajus ; but the order in both of them is quite different. The formulas, for the most part, are for the new and full-moon sacrifices; for the morning and evening fire-sacrifices; for the sacrifices to be offered every four months at the beginning of the three seasons ; for the soma-sacrifice ; for the construction of altars; for the Sautrâmanî ceremony; for the A*s*vamedha or horse-sacrifice ; for the Purushamedha or human-sacrifice ; for the Sarvamedha or universal sacrifice ; for the Pit*r*imedha or oblation to the Manes ; and for the *pravargya* or purificatory sacrifice.

The Yaju*h*-Sa*m*hitâ consists chiefly of prayers and invocations to be used at the consecration of utensils and at sacrificial ceremonials. The origin of the Yaju*h*-Sa*m*hitâ

* On the possible connexion of the Mâdhya*m*dinas with the *Madiandinoi*—see Weber's History of Indian Literature, p. 106.

† Ibid. p, 107.

‡ Ibid. pp. 34, ff.

was precisely due to circumstances like those of the Sâman; but the paraphernalia of the equally complex and highly developed ritual for which the compilation of this Veda became absolutely necessary, is more elaborate and more attractive than that of the Sâman. The Indo-Aryans gave special preference to the Yajus; for it could better satisfy their sacrificial wants than the Sâman or the *R*ik. "The Yajur-veda," says Sâya*n*a, in his Introduction to the Taittirîya-Sa*m*hitâ, "is like a wall, the two other Vedas like fresco-paintings (on it)." The history of the Yaju*h*-Sa*m*hitâ differs palpably enough from that of the other Vedas; and such difference consists in the disagreement between its own schools, which is far more weighty than the dissensions which widened the gulf between the schools of the other Vedas. These schools were founded on a division of the Yaju*h*-Sa*m*hitâ; the one party adhering to what is called the Black Yajus and the other to the White Yajus. And there is strong reason to suppose that this division must have taken place even after the time of Pâ*n*ini.* Some commentators explain *sukla* or 'white' by *suddha*.† The White Yajus is attributed to Yâjnavalkya, and the Black Yajus to Tittiri.

The Atharva-veda, though next to the *R*ik, is the most comprehensive and valuable of the four collections. The Atharvan is almost entirely a *R*ig-veda; but it has

* Goldstücker's Pâ*n*ini, p. 130 ff.

† Dvivedaganga explains शुक्लानि यजूंषि by शुद्धानि यद्वा ब्राह्मणेनाविमिश्रमन्त्रात्मकानि।

also many points of contact with the Yajus.* And there is no doubt that its songs rank chronologically with the Brâhmanas of the *R*ik, the Sâman, and the Yajus. It is more original than the last two; and consequently more interesting. Though it repeats numerous hymns of the *R*ig-veda, it contains a good many entirely new ones. This is not exactly a Veda, although many of the hymns or incantations of which it is composed, appear to be of extreme antiquity.† It was but after a hard struggle that the Atharvan came off victorious, and at last took the rank as a fourth Veda.‡ The Atharvan, however, not being used at the religious ceremonies, and chiefly containing hymns to be used at lustrations, appears to be altogether different from the other Vedas. This Veda, upon the whole, belongs to the Brahmanical period; and the songs and formulas aggregated into it also properly belonged to the Vrâtînas or unbrahmanical Aryans of the west.§ It is more like an historical than a liturgical collection. The greater portion of the Atharvan is borrowed from the last book of the *R*ik-Sa*m*hitâ.¶

* Weber's History of Indian Literature, p. 148.

† See, on the subject of this Veda, Müller's Ancient Sanskrit Literature, pp. 38, 446 ff.; Weber's History of Indian Literature, p. 10.; and Prof. Whitney's papers in the Journal of the American Oriental Society, iii. pp. 305 ff.; and iv. pp. 254 ff.

‡ Weber's History of Indian Literature, p. 11.

§ Ibid, p. 147.

¶ "By the followers of the Atharvan, the *richas*, or stanzas of the *Rig*-veda, are numerously included in their own Sa*m*hitâ (or collection)."—Sâya*n*âchârya, Introduction, Müller's edition, p. 2.

The existing Samhitâ belongs to the school of the *S*aunakas ; and to the period when Brahmanism had become dominant. There was, however, another recension of the Samhitâ belonging to the Paippalâda school. But the variations that occur in the text of the *S*aunakas are so prominent that a learned writer calls them capricious transpositions and alterations.* This collection appears to consist of complete hymns, and not of single broken and isolated verses ; and its internal arrangement is authentic. In this respect it is akin to the *R*ik, and can properly be called a complement of the first Veda, a complement containing a large mass of hymns essentially suited to its time. This Veda is called after the name of Atharvan or Athrava of the Zand-Avesta, where he is described as an itenerant preacher or preceptor. The Atharvan is divided into twenty kâ*n*das or books ; of which the last two are said to be supplementary. Of these books the first eighteen are arranged into thirty-four prapâ*t*hakas or chapters, which again contain ninety-four anuvâkas or sections ; the seventeenth book consists of only one prapâ*t*haka without any further sub-division ; the nineteenth book is not arranged into prapâ*t*hakas, but simply into seven anuvâkas ; and the twentieth consists of only nine anuvâkas, the third of which is made up of three *paryâyas*. These anuvâkas, upon the whole, embrace about six thousand verses. This Veda, perhaps, on account of the mystery which wraps up its songs, became, in no small degree, invested with a halo of sacredness, which surpassed even that of the older Vedas. From the A'thar-

* Roth's Literature and History of the Veda, p. 12.

va*n*arahasya it appears that the other three Vedas enable a man to fulfil the *dharma*, or religious law; but the Atharvan helps him to attain *moksha*, or eternal beatitude.

The Atharva-Sa*m*hitâ is rather a supplement to the *R*ig-veda than one of the four Vedas; and has very little coincidence with any of them in its general character.* It marks off the period of transition from the simple faith of the early times to the gross superstitions of the subsequent period. The Atharvan is not, however, so much of priestly as of popular origin. † It was by all means collected later than the *R*ik; and despite the fact that it has the grammatical forms of the older hymns its language conclusively proves its later origin. ‡ Its most peculiar feature consists not so much in the fact that it contains matter quite of a dissimilar character from that of the other Vedas; but as in the fact that it comprises a great number of incantations. The Atharvan is not used for the sacrifice; but embraces formulas supposed to have the influence of protecting against injurious influences of the divine powers and of the lunar asterisms too, with imprecations on enemies, prayers against diseases and noxious animals, as well as for the efficacy of healing herbs, for protection in travelling, luck in play, and such like things.§ In general, the Atharvan is poor in its hymnological and liturgical portions.

* Wilson's *R*ig-veda, i. p. viii.

† Weber's History of Indian Literature, pp. 11, 147.

‡ Roth's Dissertation on the Atharva-veda, pp. 22, ff.

§ Roth's Literature and History of the Veda, p. 12; and Whitney's Oriental and Linguistic Studies, pp. 20, f.

The first eighteen books of the Sa*m*hitâ, with which it was originally drawn up, are arranged upon one system throughout. A sixth of the bulk is not metrical; but consists of longer or shorter prose-pieces; which tally, in point of language and style, with the passages of the Brâhma*n*as. In the Atharva-veda the Bâhlikas are mentioned (v. 22, 5, 7, 14); while the *R*ig-veda is quite ignorant of such people. At any rate the oldest Indians must have been acquainted with them. There is nothing of poetical conception in the Atharvan. It is rather full of sorcery and priestly vagaries and pretensions. There is also every mark of a complete development of ritual in it. It contains no hymn addressed to Vish*n*u, nor is there any hymn addressed to Indra such as we find in the *R*ik-Sa*m*hitâ. But there is a hymn dedicated to Varu*n*a which is remarkable in every respect. This hymn formed an oath to be taken by a witness (iv. 16—comp. x. 5, 36, 44; xvi. 7, 8; xvi. 8, 1). Though there are indications of a full-blown polytheism in the Atharvan; yet there are also some traces to be found of a progress towards monotheism. As regards the authorship tradition does not afford any valuable information; but the hymns with some exceptions, are ascribed to fictitious personages. The contents of the Atharvan are a medley; but there is to be found in some books some uniformity in the subject-matter. The fourteenth book deals with marriage; the fifteenth with the glorification of Vrâtya; the sixteenth as well as the seventeenth with omens and portents; and the eighteenth with burial and the Manes-sacrifice.

The Vedas do not appear to be the productions of one

and the same author or even of the same age.* "At whatever time the work may have been performed, it constituted a decided era in the literary history of India. Thenceforth the texts became a chief object of the science and industry of the nation, as their contents had always attrac-

* It seems strange that one so well informed as Max Müller should have published the following lines: "In the most ancient Sanskrit literature, the idea even of authorship is excluded. Works are spoken of as revealed to and communicated by certain sages, but not as composed by them." *History of Ancient Sanskrit Literature, p. 523.* The earlier *R*ishis did not in any case lay claim to inspiration nor did they look upon their compositions as divinely inspired; but they knew and believed themselves simply to be the authors of the hymns of the Veda, and not to be writing by inspiration from God, as it has been alleged since they frequently speak of them as the productions of their own minds. They appear to have distinctly described themselves as the composers of the hymns. The verbs which they employ to express this idea are *kri*, "to make" (i. 184, 5; ii.39, 8; iii. 30, 20; iv.6, 11; vi. 52, 2; vii. 35, 14; viii. 51, 4; viii. 79, 3; x. 54, 6; x. 101, 2); *taksh*, "to fabricate"=the Greek *tektainomai* (i. 62, 13; i. 130, 6; ii. 19, 8; ii. 35, 2, v. 2, 11; v. 29, 15; vi. 32, 1; vii. 7, 6. viii. 6, 33; x. 39, 14; x. 80, 7); and *jan* "to beget," or "produce" (iii. 2, 1; vii. 15, 4; vii. 22, 9; viii. 43, 2; viii. 77, 4; viii. 84, 4, 5; ix. 73, 2; x. 67, 1) Nevertheless the *R*ishis were not altogether unconscious of higher influences (iii. 37, 4); and they seem to have attached a high value to their productions, which, as they believed, were acceptable to the gods (v. 45, 4; v. 85, 1; vii. 26, 1, 2; x. 23, 6; x. 54, 6; x. 105, 8). There are also a great multitude of passages in the *R*ik which ascribe a supernatural character to the earlier *R*ishis (vii. 76, 4; iii. 53, 9; vii. 33, 11 ff; vii. 87. 4; vii. 88, 3 ff; x. 14, 15; x. 62, 4, 5); and even to the hymns (i. 37, 4; iii. 18, 3; vii. 34, 1; vii, 34, 9; x. 176, 2). There are similar passages to be met with in Homer and Hesiod. The *R*ishis are said to have held intercourse about sacred truths with the gods (i. 179, 2; vii. 76, 4). Again, on the other hand, some among them professed their ignorance of all matters either human or divine (i. 164, 5). There are many hymns in which it appears also that the consciousness of some affinity with the divine nature was uppermost in their mind; and they likewise believed to have been en-

ted its highest reverence and admiration ; and so thorough and religious was the care bestowed upon their preservation, that, notwithstanding their mass and the thousands of

dowed with superior wisdom, and to have possessed the knowledge of the deities. (i. 31, 1 ; iii. 21, 3 ; v. 29, 1 ; vi. 14, 2 ; viii. 6, 41 ; ix. 107, 7 ; x. 115, 5). When the idea both of inspiration and of independent composition is at the same time traceable in the *Rik-Samhitâ*, it is possible that the notion of inspiration may not have occupied the minds of the earlier sages ; but may have grown up among their successors, or more properly that it may have been entertained by some and not by all of them. The *Rishis* sought from their gods every kind of temporal blessings, such as long life, food, riches, strength, offspring, cattle and rain. And they in like manner expected that those gods would direct their devotional acts, stimulate their poetical powers, and inspire them to compose hymns in honor of them. Hence we see the most distinct indications in some of the hymns of superhuman character ascribed to the *Rishis* themselves, and of divine influence which suggested their compositions (Muir's Sanskrit Texts, iii. p. 252). But when the Vedas mellowed into inspired scripturehood we are not now in a position to say even approximately. The claims as to the divine and infallible character of the Vedas must have been set up gradually. But a protest seems to have been made by the Buddhists against such claims during the Sûtra period (compare Yâska's Nirukta, i. 15). And it is also manifest that the reverence for the Vedas must have been on the wane before the days of Yâska and Pâṇini (Pâṇini. iv. 4, 60). The Indian authors shortly before, or subsequent to, the collectien of the Vaidik writings held the opinions on the origin of the Vedas, as springing from the mystical sacrifice of Purusha, *Rig-veda*, x. 90, 9 ; as resting on Skambha, *Atharva-veda*, x. 7, 14 ; as springing from Indra, xiii. 4, 38 ; as produced from time, xix. 54, 3 ; as produced from Agni, Vâyu, and Sûrya, *Manu*, i. 21-23, and *Satapatha-Brâhmana*, xi. 5, 8, 1 ff. ; as springing from Prajâpati, and the waters, *Satapatha-Brâhmana*, vi. 1, 1, 8 ; as springing from the leavings of the sacrifice (uchchhishta), *Atharva-veda*, xi. 7, 24 ; as issued from the mouth of Brahmâ at the creation, *Vishnu-Purâna*, i. 5, 48 ff., *Bhâgavata-Purâna*, iii. 12, 34 and 37ff., and *Mârkandeya-Purâna*, 102, 1 ; as created by Brahmâ, or as produced from the Gâyatrî, *Harivansa*, verses 47, and 11,516 ; as created by Vishnu, or as having Sarasvatî for their years which have elapsed since their collection, hardly a single various reading, so far as is yet known, has been suffered to make its way into them after their definite and final establishment. The influence which they have exerted upon the whole literary development of after ages is not easily to be rated too high."*

All that is not found of the oldest Veda in the Sâman and the Yajus, is a *R*ik piece-meal ; its hymns broken into parts ; verses from different hymns assembled anew ; and even the composition of numerous parts aggregated into the same songs, as if they had the same author. That under such circumstances, the Yajus should have lost its interest so far as poetry is concerned, was only to be expected ; it is, however, a curious fact, that the Sâman has preserved so much of that beauty which so peculiarly marks the *R*ig-veda poetry. The Atharvan, too, is composed in like manner as the Yajus, with only some variants, so that the additions in it to the mutilated extracts from the *R*ik, are more considerable than those in the Yajus.

There exists no record that carries us back to a more

mother, *Mahâbhârata*, *Sântiparvan*, *verse* 12,920 ; and a passage in the Taittirîya-Brâhmana speaks of the Veda as being "the hair of Prajâpati's beard." iii. 39, 1, etc., etc. In like manner, many other authorities might be cited to the same effect ; but they are also puerile and contradictory in themselves. The *R*ishis designated the older hymns, and the more recent ones by various names, such as *arka*, *uktha*, *rich*, *gir*, *dhî*, *nîitha*, *nivid*, *mantra*, *mati*, *sûkta*, *stoma*, *vâch*, *vachas*, *sâman*, *yajus*, *manman*, *manîshâ*, *sumati*, *dhîti*, *dhishanâ*, *stutî*, *samsa*, *sushtuti*, *prasasti*, *etc.*, *etc.*; and they also often applied to them the title of *brahma* which has also the sense of hymn or prayer (iv. 16, 21 ; v. 29, 15 ; vi. 17, 13 ; vi. 50, 6 ; vii. 61, 6, x. 89, 3).

* Whitney's Oriental and Linguistic Studies, p. 22.

primitive state of the human family than the *Ri*g-veda. And the few relics that have been preserved to us, are of most intense interest. It has been very appropriately said that there is one oasis in the vast desert of ancient Asiatic history, and it is the only real Veda, the *Ri*g-veda, the earliest existing literary record of the whole Aryan race.* The priority of the *Ri*k to all the other Vedas is thoroughly established by the fact that its numerous hymns are repeated in them; and that its *Ri*shis are referred to even in the Atharvan. But in the Atharvan the names of the *Ri*shis thus produced, are principally of the more recent *Ri*shis; while those in the *Ri*k are of the greatest antiquity.† In the Atharvan a more developed state of the institutions together with the caste system appears than what we find in the *Ri*k. In the former we see the people bound hand and foot by the fetters of a wily and tyrannical hierarchy and superstition; while in the latter we find them quite free, and imbued with a warm love of nature. Judging from the language and internal character of the Atharvan, we arrive at the conclusion that the main body of this Veda was in existence at a time when the *Ri*k was compiled. In the White Yaju*h* Sa*m*hitâ an enumeration is given of the different classes of men who are to be consecrated at the Purushamedha, and of the names of most of the mixed castes. We may, therefore, conclude that the Brahmanical element had then gained the supremacy, and the system of caste was completely organised.‡

* Müller's Chips from a German Workshop i. p. 5.

† Roth's Literature and History of the Veda, p. 13.

‡ Weber's History of Indian Literature p. 111.

The 90th hymn of the tenth book of the *Rig*-veda is entitled the Purusha-sûkta; which also occurs in the 31st book of the Vâjasaneyi-Samhitâ (1-16), and in the 19th book of the Atharva-veda (6, 1ff.) There it is said that the Brahman, Kshattriya, Vaisya did not issue respectively from the mouth, arms, and thighs of Purusha; but simply the Brahman was his mouth, the Râjanya was made his arms, the Vaisya was his thighs, and the *S*ûdra only sprang from his feet.* The text thus conclusively proves that there was no caste; but there were only four different classes of people. The fact that the Sâman has not extracted any verse from it, is not without meaning.† The opening parts of the *Sûkta* are of a pantheistic character; and the whole of it contains allusions to the sacrificial ceremonials, and not to the actual immolation of a human victim. In it, the sacrifice is not offered to the gods but by the gods themselves. Nor are there human priests mentioned; and the Purusha could not have been an ordinary man. It is full of technical and philosophical terms; and contains certain modern words such as *S*ûdra, Râjanya Vaisya, Sâdhyas and prishadâjya; and there is also mention made of the three seasons—spring, summer and autumn, which do not occur in any other hymn. A reference is also made to the four different kinds of Vaidik compositions such as *r*ik, sâman, chhandas, and yajus, which distinctly proves the comparatively later date of the *Sûkta*. And, no doubt, here the Atharvan is referred to under the appellation of *Chhandas*. From these facts it is apparent that

* Mahâbhârata, iii. 12,962.

† Weber's Indische Studien, ix. p. 3.

it belongs to the close of the Vaidik age; and it is also found scarcely to enunciate any uniform, orthodox and authoritative doctrine in regard to the four-fold origin of the human race.*

The various hymns of the *R*ik-Sa*m*hitâ were composed by various *R*ishis. Each hymn is said to have had its *R*ishi; and these *R*ishis comprise a variety of secular as well as religious individuals, who became famous at different times in Indian tradition. The primitive traditions, though few, are yet sufficient to prove that in the Vaidik age the capacity for metrical composition, and the highest prerogative of officiating at the worship of the gods, were not regarded as exclusively confined to individuals of priestly caste. Even females are spoken of as authors of hymns or parts of hymns, as Romasâ, daughter of B*r*ihaspati (i. 126), Lopamudrâ (i. 179, 1), and Visvavârâ, of the family of Atri (v. 28). And it is also a very remarkable and curious fact that we find one Kavasha Ailûsha, himself a *S*ûdra,† to have composed a few of the Sûktas in the tenth book of the *R*ig-veda. The epithets applied by the authors of the hymns to themselves and to the sages who in earlier times had appointed, as well as to their contemporaries who followed them in conducting, the different rites at the worship of the gods, are the following; *rishi*, *kavi*, *medhâvin*, *vipra*, *vipaschit*, *vedhas*, *muni*, etc. The Vedas are said to have been perpetuated by oral tradition, until they were collected and arranged by a school or

* Muir's Original Sanskrit Texts, i. pp. 7-15; Colebrooke's Essays, i. p. 309, note; Müller's History of Ancient Sanskrit Literature, pp. 570, f.

† Aitareya-Brâhmana, ii. 19; Kaushîtaki-Brâhmana, xi.

schools of learned Brahmans of which the nominal head was Krishna Dvaipâyana Vyâsa, the Indian Pisistratus.* Vyâsa, who flourished in the early part of the twelfth century B. C.,† having collected and arranged with others the so-called revealed scriptures, taught them to some of his disciples, *viz.*, the *R*ik to Paila, the Yajus to Vaisampâyana, the Sâman to Jaimini, and the Atharvan to Sumantu; and they in like manner taught to their disciples, who again in their turn communicated their knowledge to their pupils.‡

The Vedas are written in an ancient form of Sanskrit; which is to the later what Chaucer's writings are to modern English. They abound in obsolete and peculiar expressions made up of the more recent grammatical forms with such irregularity as leads to the inference that the language was too unsettled and variable to be brought under subjection to a system of rigid grammatical rules.

The Vaidik dialect is to be understood as the least altered representative of that original tongue from which are descended the languages of the leading races of Asia and Europe. The dialect of the first three Vedas is very ancient and at the same time very difficult. When it is compared with the classical Sanskrit it appears that both

* Lassen's Indian Antiquities, i. p. 777, note; and also Mahábhárata, i. 2417 and 4236.

† Archdeacon Pratt's Letter on Colebrooke's Determination of the Date of the Veda, in the Journal of the Asiatic Society of Bengal, 1862, vol. xxxi. pp. 49 seq.; and Journal of the American Oriental Society, viii. pp. 83.

‡ Weber's Vájasaneyi-Samhitá, p. 1; Colebrooke's Essays, i. p. 14; and Wilson's *R*ig-veda, i. p. xx.

are phonetically and grammatically very far from being the same, and lexically they are as wide as possible. "The language of the Vedas is an older dialect, varying very considerably, both in its grammatical and lexical character, from the classical Sanskrit. Its grammatical peculiarities run through all departments : euphonic rules, word-formation and composition, declension, conjugation, syntax. . . . . [These peculiarities] are partly such as characterize an older language, consisting in a greater originality of forms, and the like, and partly such as characterize a language which is still in the bloom and vigour of life, its freedom untrammelled by other rules than those of common usage, and which has not, like the (classical) Sanskrit, passed into oblivion as a native spoken dialect, become merely a conventional medium of communication among the learned, being forced, as it were, into a mould of regularity by long and exhausting grammatical treatment. . . . . . The dissimilarity existing between the two, in respect of the stock of words of which each is made up, is, to say the least, not less marked. Not single words alone, but whole classes of derivations and roots, with the families that are formed from them, which the Veda exhibits in frequent and familiar use, are wholly wanting, or have left but faint traces, in the classical dialect; and this to such an extent as seems to demand, if the two be actually related to one another directly as mother and daughter, a longer interval between them than we should be inclined to assume, from the character and degree of the grammatical, and more especially the phonetic, differences."*

* Journal of the American Oriental Society, iii. pp. 296, ff.

The chronology of the Vaidik age is indicated in the different styles of composition which are to be met with in the Vedas as well as in the Brâhma*n*as and the Sûtras. The Vaidik age is divided by Müller into four distinct periods: namely, the Chhandas period, the Mantra period, the Brâhma*n*a period, and the Sûtra period. The respective styles of composition of these four periods seem to differ very much from one another. In the Chhandas period the oldest hymns were composed; and this period in fact furnishes us with a fair picture of the primitive society of the Indo-Aryans at a time when no particular system of religion was prevalent. Even sacrifices were not then in vogue. But in the Mantra period they came to be held in great estimation; and in this period the more recent hymns were composed, and the whole was placed together and arranged into one Sa*m*hitâ. Three other Sa*m*hitâs were also collected and arranged systematically for a distinct theological or sacrificial purpose. At this time there were priests by profession, who had elaborated a most highly complex system of sacrifices. In the Brâhma*n*a period the principal theological and liturgical books bearing this title were composed and marshalled together; and theological speculations were much indulged in. In the Sûtra period the ceremonial precepts of the earlier times were reduced to a systematic form. The works of this period were not all written in the enigmatical form of Sûtras, but some were in verse and others in prose. The Vedas have their own Brâhma*n*as and Sûtras; and as the Sûtras presuppose the Brâhma*n*as, and the Brâhma*n*as do not refer to them, it is proved that the Brâhmana period must have preceded the Sûtra period. In the Brâhmana and Sûtra periods the Sanskrit language must have undergone considerable modifications. The Sûtra period extends far into the Buddhistic times ; and we can place this period on the frontier of the Vaidik age. In this period certainly occurred one of the most remarkable changes in the Indo-Aryan religion and society.

The Chhandas period may be supposed, according to Max Müller, to have lasted from 1200 to 1000 B. C.; the Mantra period from 1000 to 800 B. C. ; the Brâhmana period from 800 to 600 B. C. ; and the Sûtra period from 600 to 200 B. C. "To decide the question," says Barthélémy Saint-Hilaire, "with absolute certainty as to the dates of these four periods of ancient Sanskrit literature, would be impossible ; for Indian literature itself is almost without known dates, owing either to the peculiar organisation of the Hindu mind, or to the convulsions of Indian society. The present condition of Sanskrit philology does not afford the scholar the requisite data for embarking with any chance of success in such chronological speculations. Uncertainty hangs over these periods ; and to assign an approximate length to each of these periods is altogether hazardous. It should be well understood that these dates are only approximately accurate ; and notwithstanding the apparent accuracy of the figures, it is clear that one cannot in this case arrive at any precise conclusion. Moreover, Max Müller would perhaps have done better, if he had not sought to fix such precise limits to write down the result of his investigations so accurately. As there is necessarily always much vagueness in calculations of this nature, it is well that the form given to hypotheses be just as vague as our data ; and as there is nothing so certain as a number once pronounced, I think it would have been better to remain partly in the dark, which in fact, is quite excusable in such matters. Besides, every body will see that the chronological limits assigned by Max Müller to the four periods of Vaidik literature are too narrow rather than too wide. The same conviction has been expressed by Professor Wilson and Dr. Whitney. If Max Müller is wanting in any thing it is chiefly through an excess of reserve. The period of the Sa*m*hitâs, such as we now possess, is dated at least 1000 years before the Christian era. One may, without the slightest hesitation, place the period of the Chhandas far beyond that. Then again one alights upon the calculations of Sir William Jones, and of Colebrooke, who assigned to the composition of the *R*ig-veda a period fourteen or fifteen hundred years before Christ.

In another point of view, this uniform length of two centuries assigned to the period of the Brâhma*n*as, as well as to that of the Mantras and of the Chhandas, is equally open to criticism. If the period of the Sûtras comprised four entire centuries, it seems hardly probable that the period of the Brâhma*n*as which are quite as long and perhaps equally numerous, should not have extended over a longer time, including the A'ra*n*yakas and the Upanishads. Moreover there is certainly a far smaller interval between the Brâhma*n*as and the Sûtras, than there is between the Mantras and the Brâhma*n*as. Nevertheless Max Müller reckons only two centuries between each of these two periods. Analogy would seem to authorize the assumption of a far longer interval between the latter two than between the former two. There is an immense difference between the period assigned to the collection of sacred poetry, and the period in which they are commented upon ; there is a smaller difference between this latter epoch and the one in which these manifold and obscure commentaries are reduced to clear and orderly rules. As for the period of the Mantras, it seems in its turn too extensive, if that of the Brâhma*n*as is not sufficiently so. Granted that two centuries had been necessary for the composition of the Brâhma*n*as, the simple collection of the Sa*m*hitâs did not require so much time. Thus, without contesting the absolute length of the united periods, their relative lengths do not seem to be very acceptable, and their proportions might be settled in a totally different manner, which could be equally justified. As for the period of the Chhandas, the first of all, and the most fertile, since it has rendered all the rest comparatively worthless, it is to be presumed that it was the longest ; and this inspiration, which, during more than three thousand years, has enlivened the entire religious creed of a great people, cannot have been of so short a duration, since its effects are so durable."

First of all were composed the hymns, and then the Brâhma*n*as. It is, therefore, possible that several centuries intervened between the composition of both the hymns and the Brâhma*n*as, as a not inconsiderable space of time must have been required for the literal meaning and purport of the hymns becoming somewhat obscure and doubtful, and invested with a halo of sacredness. In the same manner the period during which the Brâhma*n*as were drawn up must have been separated from that of the Sûtras by several centuries, as a sufficient space of time must have elapsed for further modification of language, and the growth of a new theology which claimed for the Brâhma*n*as the same sacredness which the Brâhma*n*as themselves did for the hymns. There are however no sufficient data by which we can determine with precision the period during which the hymns were composed. The hymns are divided into two classes, the Mantras or more recent hymns which according to some scholars may have been produced between 1000 and 800 years before the Christian era; and the Chhandas or the older hymns which, they suppose, may have been composed between 1200 and 1000 B. C. Other scholars hold altogether a different opinion; * and it is shared by Dr. Haug who writes thus: "We do not hesitate, therefore, to assign the composition of the bulk of the Brâhma*n*as to the years 1400-1200 B. C.; for the Sa*m*hitâ we require a period of *at least* 500-600 years, with an interval of about two hundred years between the end of the proper Brâhma*n*a period. Thus we obtain for the bulk of Sa*m*hitâ the space from 1400-2000; the oldest hymns and sacrificial formulas may be a few hundred years more ancient still, so that we would fix the very commencement of Vaidik literature between 2000-2400 B. C."† The chronological distance of the Vaidik age is to be measured not

* Müller's Ancient Sanskrit Literature, p. 572; and his edition of the *R*ig-veda, iv. pp. iv.-xiii.

† Haug's Aitareya-Brâhma*n*a, i. p. 47.

merely by the revolutions and progress of the heavenly bodies ; but also by the revolutions and progress of the human mind. We do not see any reason why there should be altogether a distinct era for the Chhandas when it may be held as the same with the Mantra period which undoubtedly included the new, intermediate and ancient hymns.* However, there are no mile-stones in Vaidik literature. The classification of ancient Sanskrit literature has now become a theme for discussion by every Sanskrit scholar. But where it is to end is not easy to surmise. It has been questioned whether the basis of that classification is scientific or ritual or theological. But whatever may be advanced against such an arrangement, we have every reason to place our faith in the distribution of Vaidik litereture into distinct periods.

* Wilson's Works, v. p. 337 ; Haug's Aitareya-Brâhmana, i. p. 23 ; and Goldstücker's Pânini, p. 71.

CHAPTER IV.

The Division of the Vedas into Mantras and Brâhmanas—the proper meaning of Sâkhâ, Charana, and Parishad—the A'ranyakas—the Upanishads—and the Distinction between Sruti and Smriti.

THE division of the Vedas is two-fold, Mantras and Brâhmanas.* Such a division is indeed an essential one especially when it separates two different classes of writings, which are related to one another as canonized text on the one hand, and canonized explanation on the other. That part of each Veda which contains the mantras—the metrical hymns or prose forms of prayer, is called its Sa*m*hitâ; and this definition applies equally to all the Sa*m*hitâs except that of the Black Yajur Veda, in which both the Mantra and the Brâhma*n*a portions are combined. But yet it is to be believed that this Sa*m*hitâ had a separate

* Sâya*n*a says in his commentary on the *R*ig-veda: "The definition (of the Veda) as a book composed of *mantra* and *brâhmana*, is unobjectionable. Hence A'pastamba says in the Yajnaparibhâshâ, 'Mantra and Brâhma*n*a have the name of Veda.'"

Brâhma*n*a annexed to it.* The Brâhma*n*as stand to the Mantras in the same relation as the Talmud does to the Mosaic code. The former presuppose the earlier existence of the latter; and the proof that the Mantras are far older than any other portion of Indian literature, is to be found particularly in the character of their language. Though the Mantras and the Brâhma*n*as were held at a later period to have existed together, it admits of no question that the Brâhma*n*a portion of each Veda is posterior at least to some part of its Sa*m*hitâ; for the former evidently refers to, and contains extracts from the latter.† And it needs scarcely be stated that so large a collection of works including both the portions must have been the gradual product of several centuries. Indeed, they represent various mutations of society, various phases of religious belief, and even different periods of language. The difficulty in distinguishing these periods is however immensely increased by the apparent losses, which these writings must have sustained before they were aggregated together and preserved in the shape in which we now find them. The Mantras and the Brâhma*n*as had to pass through a large number of *S*âkhâs;

* Müller's History of Ancient Sanskrit Literature, p. 350; and Weber's History of Indian Literature, p. 83.

† On the subject of the priority of the hymns to the Brâhma*n*as the commentator of the Taittiriya, or Black Yajur-veda, Sa*m*hitâ, thus delivers himself:—"Although the Veda is formed both of Mantra and Brâhma*n*a, yet as the Brâhma*n*a consists of an explanation of the Mantras, it is the latter which were at first recorded" (p. 9 of the Calcutta edition). Sáya*n*a in his commentary on the Brihad-A'ra*n*yaka Upanishad also says that "the Mantras are the sources of the Brâhma*n*as."—Bibliotheca Indica, ii. pp. 855, ff.

and consequently the dissensions, which sprang up among those schools, either in connexion with the Vaidik texts or their interpretations were very bitter. The Mantras are generally in verse, whilst the Brâhmanas are entirely in prose. The Mantras, in fact, were for ages unwritten, and the elliptical style of their composition is the only evidence of their oral transmission.

Most of the Brâhmanas are collective works ; and there are old and new Brâhmanas. But those that have now perished, are found in diverse manner quoted or referred to. They were, in fact, the productions of the schools of the Brahmanic priesthood. Though they are puerile, and in the main tediously prolix, verbose and artificial, yet they are found to contain much important matter both theological and ceremonial. We also find in them the oldest rituals, the oldest linguistic expositions, the oldest legendary narratives, and the oldest philosophical and mystical speculations all of which are mixed up with each other. But they seem to differ widely from one another in point of details ; and this is simply owing to the fact that they belong to one or the other of the Vedas. With respect to their origin and age they occupy a kind of intermediate position between the transition from a simple Vaidik mode of thought to the Brahmanical vagaries.* And this transition was indeed brought about solely by the Brâhmanas themselves. They were drawn up with a view to enforce various ceremonies and sacrifices, to illustrate the use of the hymns at them, and to enjoin the duties of the

* Weber's History of Indian Literature, p. 12.

different classes of priests. The authors, however, generally failed to understand the rational meaning of the hymns, and so suggested the most absurd explanations of the various formularies which of course had originally some reasonable drift. The number of the old Brâhma*nas* must have been very considerable as every *S*âkhâ consisted of a Sa*m*hitâ and a Brâhma*na*. It must not, therefore, be supposed that the Brâhma*nas* were not all composed independently by different authors. Each Brâhma*na* is included in its own Veda, and is ascribed to no human author. The different Brâhma*nas* in fact obtained their names from the schools by which they were transmitted. For the *R*ig-veda we have the Aitareya, and the *S*ânkhâyana or Kaushîtaki ; for the Sâma-veda, the Prau*d*ha, the Sha*d*vin*sa*, the Sâmavidhi, etc ; for the White Yajur-veda the *S*atapatha ; for the Black Yajur-veda the Taittirîya ; and for the Atharva-veda the Gopatha. The Brâhma*nas* of the *R*ik generally prescribe the duties of the Hot*r*is. The Brâhma*nas* of the Sâman specify the duties of the Udgât*r*is ; and the Brâhma*nas* of the Yajus confine themselves to the duties of the Adhvaryus.

A Brâhma*na* was originally a theological tract, and it was so designated because it owed its origin to *brahman* or prayer.* The entire collection of Brâhma*nas* gives the impression of having undergone a secondary alteration ;

* Instead of slaying the slain over again, we quote the following words of Haug :—The word brahma or brahman is the most important word of Hindu theology and philosophy. Brahma occurs twice in the Nighan*t*avas or the *glôssai*, as a name for *"food"* (Annanâma 2, 7), and for *"riches"* (dhananâma 2, 10). In Sâya*n*a's commentary on the hymns of the *R*ig-veda it is sometimes explained with reference to this signification, and sometimes

and their prevalence constitutes a distinct stage in the progress of the religious history of the Indo-Aryans. As the dogmatical books of the Brahmans they contain a system of tenets, which were of necessity the result of religious practice. If they do not afford a rational explanation of the principles of belief, they are still very useful for such an exposition, because they were composed with the distinct object of explaining and establishing the whole sacrificial

in other ways, *ex. gr.*, (1) food, in general, 1, 10, 4 ; more frequently, sacrificial food as in 4, 22, 1 ; (2) performance of the song of the Soma singers, 7, 35, 7 ; (3) magic, charm, spell, 2, 23, 1 ; (4) ceremonies, having a song of praise as their characteristic ; (5) performance of song and sacrifice 7, 23, 1 ; (6) the recitation of the Hotri priests ; (7) great, 6, 23, 1. These all seem to point to the principal meanings, namely, "food," in particular "*sacrificial food*," and the performance of the song at the sacrifice. The meaning "*devotion*" given to the word "brahma" is quite inapplicable. In the language of the Avesta we find, as far as sound is concerned, an absolutely identical word, namely *baresman*. By it the Pársis understand a regularly cut bundle of twigs tied together with grass, and used at their Fire-ceremonies exactly as the little clipped bundle of kusa grass is used by Brahmans, at the Soma sacrifices. This latter is called Veda (A'svaláyana, Srauta-Sûtra, 1,11) which passes later as a synonym of brahma. This bunch of grass as well as the baresman has a symbolical meaning. They both represent growing, increase, prosperity. The original meaning of the word was growth. Hence came the meaning "prosperity," "success." As the success of the sacrifice entirely depended upon the holy texts, the chanting, the sacrificial forms and offerings, the word could be used for any one of these essentials. As the chanting of the hymns of praise was the most important of these the word was most frequently employed in this sense. As sacrifice with the Vaidik Indians was the chief means to obtain all earthly and spiritual blessings, but was itself useless without the brahma *i. e.* success, the latter was at last regarded as the original cause of all beings.—Haug, Brahma und die Brahmanen, p. 5ff ; Muir's Original Sanskrit Texts, i. pp. 240-65.

ceremonial. They exhibit, upon the whole, a distinct phase in the intellectual history of the Indo-Aryans; but in a literary point of view, they are altogether without any interest. They are in the main marked by sober reasoning, full of genuine thoughts, lofty expressions, and valuable traditions; but their general characteristics mainly consist in their archaisms, grammatical irregularities, antiquated and tautological style and antiquarian pedantry. In them we find a pantheistic system; and this system was adopted simply for the explanation of the Vaidik deities. There also occur numerous tales of the battles between the Devas and the Asuras, which are to be understood as traditional reminiscences of the hostilities between the Indo-Aryans and the Assyrians during their wanderings in Asia before the Indian immigration. Even there the Brahman, the Kshattriya, the Vai*s*ya, and the *S*ûdra are repeatedly named by their proper appellations; and their peculiar offices and relative stations are also clearly discriminated.

The Gopatha-Brâhma*n*a of the Atharva-veda is the Veda of the Bh*r*igu-angiras; which does not properly belong to the sacred literature of the Indo-Aryans. This Brâhma*n*a is of a small size. Its language is similar to that of the other Brâhma*n*as. Nothing is treated of in it in all its details; and even the manner in which every topic is discussed is by no means interesting. The primary object of this Brâhma*n*a is to show and establish the importance and also the efficacy of the four Vedas. The Purvârdha, or the first part of it, comprises five prapâ*th*akas; and the other part, called the Uttarârdha, consists of six prapâ*th*akas. The customary ceremonial of worship is discussed in it in like manner as in the other Brâhmanas; and there is, indeed, very little difference to be seen between the Gopatha and those Brâhmanas. It begins with a theory of the creation of the universe as do the other Brâhmanas. It deals with the importance of *âchamana*, the rules regarding *dikshâ*, the mystic connexion of the year with ceremonies, the creation and requirements of ceremonies, the morning, noon, and evening rites and other minor sacrifices. It is also remarkable on account of the chapter of accidents. It was composed after the schism of the Charakas and the Vâjasaneyins* and the completion of the Vâjasaneyi-Samhitâ; and we must at any rate assign to it a later date than to the Brâhmanas of the other Vedas. It was written probably about six centuries B. C. The number of Brâhmanas belonging to the Sâma-veda, is eight; and their names are: the Praudha or Mahâ-Brâhmana (*i.e.*, the Tândya or Panchavinsa) the Shadvinsa, the Sâmavidhi, the A'rsheya, the Devatâdhyâya, the Vansa, the Samhitopanishad, and the Upanishad,† which probably is the Chhândogya-Upanishad, and is thus ranked among the Brâhmanas.‡ The A'rsheya-Brâhmana is an Anukramanî consisting of three and a half prapâthakas. It is found in both the recensions of the Kauthumas and the Jaiminîyas; but the latter differs considerably from the former. This Brâhmana is devoted to an enumeration of the Seers of the

* Müller's History of Ancient Sanskrit Literature, pp. 451, ff; and see also Mitra's Gopatha-Brâhmana, pp. 11-37.

† Müller's History of Ancient Sanskrit Literature, p. 349.

‡ Müller's Rig-veda, i. p. xxvii.

Sâman. The Devatâdhyâya is composed of four khandas. It embraces some miscellaneous fragments both old and new; but has no literary value. This Brâhmana contains philological speculations regarding the names of some Vaidik metres, and also shows some traces of the Buddhist influences. The Vansa is full of myths and legends of great value. This Brâhmana is also called an Anukramanî; and it is similar in character to the A'rsheya. The Tândya-Brâhmana, also called the Panchavinsa, contains twenty-five books; and treats chiefly of Soma sacrifice. It contains also minute descriptions of the sacrifices performed on the banks of the Sarasvatî and Drishadvatî; and of the Vrâtyastomas or sacrifices by which such Aryans as were against Brahmanical polity, had admission to the Brahman community. This Brâhmana is also extremely rich in legendary contents as well as in information of a general nature; but, upon the whole, its contents are very dry. It was contemporary with, or even anterior to the flourishing epoch of the kingdom of the Kurupanchâlas.* The Shadvinsa-Brâhmana, which is a supplement to the Panchavinsa, treats of expiatory sacrifices and imprecatory ceremonies. It is supposed to be of very modern date. And it not only alludes to temples but also to the images of the gods. The Sâmavidhi is in three chapters; and is of a highly artificial character, and presents no feature of interest. It appears that this Brâhmana has undergone some rearrangement, and belongs to a movement which resulted in the philosophies of Kumârila and Sankara. The subject-matter is nothing else than

* Weber's History of Indian Literature, p. 68.

the description of certain penances and ceremonies which are altogether of little value. There is, however, mention made of ceremonies some of which are meant for the expiation of sins and crimes ; and in fact there was then no distinction between them.* We are therefore warranted to conclude that it contains the germs of the criminal law of later times.† Burnell assigns to this Brâhma*n*a in its present form not a higher antiquity than the fifth century B. C.‡ A later Brâhma*n*a probably of modern date, and which is not mentioned by Sâya*n*a, is the Adbhuta-Brâhma*n*a. It treats of evil occurences of daily life, omens and portents.

The Chhândogya-Brâhma*n*a of the Sâma-veda, of which the Chhândogya-Upanishad constitutes a part, comprises ten prapâ*t*hakas ; of these the first two are called the Chhândogya-mantra-Brâhma*n*a, and the rest forms the Chhândogya-Upanishad. Of the two chapters of the Chhândogya-Brâhma*n*a the first embraces eight *sûktas* on the ceremony of marriage, and the ceremonies to be performed at the birth of a child. The second chapter includes eight *sûktas*, which are consecrated to the Earth, Agni, and Indra. It also contains mantras for offering oblations to the Manes, Sûrya, and various other deities very often united with a prayer for wealth, health, and prosperity. The concluding mantra has reference to the marriage ceremony. This Brâhma*n*a contains also a mass of highly interesting legends indicating the gradual

* Maine's Ancient Law, p. 371.

† Burnell's Sâmavidhâna, p. xvff.

‡ Ibid, p. x.

development of Brahmanic theology. The Aitareya-Brâhmana originated in the country of the Kurupanchâlas and Vasa-Usînaras. This Brâhmana is one of the collections of the sayings of ancient Brahmâ priests explanatory of the sacred duties of the so-called Hotri priests. Its style is throughout uniform. The greater part of the work appears to have been written by one and the same author; some additions, however, were made afterwards. This Brâhmana and the Sânkhâyana or Kaushîtaki-Brâhmana are closely connected with each other; but there are points of divergence in the distribution of their matter. Though they treat essentially of the same matter, their views of the same question often appear to be antagonistic. The Aitareya contains eight panchikâs or pentades, divided into forty adhyâyas or lectures, which again are sub-divided into 285 khandas or portions; but the last ten adhyâyas are but a later addition to it. This work treats chiefly of Soma sacrifice. The Sânkhâyana is a perfectly arranged work, and consists of thirty adhyâyas, likewise sub-divided into a number of khandas. It embraces the complete sacrificial procedure. This Brâhmana originated simultaneously with the last few books of the Samhitâ of the White Yajus. It also appears that the first thirty adhyâyas of the Aitareya-Brâhmana are older than those of the Sânkhâyana.*

The Satapatha-Brâhmana, according to the Mâdhyamdina school, is divided into 14 kândas or books, which contain 100 adhyâyas or lectures; or into 68 prapâthakas, with 438 brâhmanas, and 7624 kandikâs or portions. In the

* Goldstücker's Literary Remains, i. p. 35.

Kâ*n*va recension it consists of seventeen kâ*nd*as with a hundred and four adhyâyas, four hundred and forty-six brâhma*n*as, and five thousand eight hundred and sixty-six ka*nd*ikâs. This Brâhma*n*a furnishes us with the dogmatical, exegetical, mystical, and philosophical lucubrations of early Brahman theologians and philosophers. A partial examination of this book shows it to be stamped with a character quite in harmony with that of the Aitareya. And again these two works have claims to be recognized as very ancient records of the religious beliefs and rituals, and of the pristine institutions of Indian society. A story in the *S*atapatha illustrates the relations between the priestly and royal families in the early history of India; and gives us an insights into the policy which actuated the Brahmans to struggle from time to time for political influence. There is also a legend of a deluge, in which Manu alone was preserved for his sanctity and superior wisdom. According to this interesting legend he was not the creator of man, but a representative of an earlier race of men.* The legend of a flood, according to M. Burnouf, is not in its origin Indian, but was most probably derived from a Semitic source, whether Hebrew or Assyrian.† But Prof. Weber from the legend of Manu in the *S*atapatha-Brâhma*n*a, which he for the first time brought to light has proved that the tradition was really current in India at a

* i. 8, 1, 1. See also Müller's Ancient Sanskrit Literature, pp. 425ff; Professor Williams' Indian Epic Poetry, p. 34; and Weber's Indische Studien, i. 163 f.

† Bhâgavata-Purâ*n*a, iii. pp. li., lii.-liv.

much earlier period than Burnouf thought; and it was not imported into that country from any of the Semitic sources.* This Brâhma*n*a may have been edited by Yâjnavalkya, but its principal portions, like those of the other Brâhma*n*as, must have been accumulating for some period before they were all aggregated and arranged into the sacred code of a new Chara*n*a. The Taittirîya-Brâhma*n*a may be regarded as a supplement to its Sa*m*hitâ; but the former does not differ from the latter so much in character as in point of time.

There was originally only one text of each of the four Vedas; but each text passed through a large number of *S*âkhâs which gradually came into existence. A *S*âkhâ signifies an edition of a Veda. There was a class of *S*âkhâs, though of a confessedly later date, founded on Sûtras, which derived their names from historical personages. However, there was originally a difference between a *S*âkhâ and a Chara*n*a; but these two words were used generally as synonyms. Pâ*n*ini speaks of Chara*n*as as comprising a number of followers.† If a *S*âkhâ is used in the sense of a Chara*n*a, this can only be accounted for by the fact that in India the *S*âkhâs did not exist not as written books, but only in the tradition of the Chara*n*as, each member of a Chara*n*a representing and possessing a copy of a book. A *S*âkhâ as a portion of *S*ruti, cannot properly include law books. But the adherents of certain *S*âkhâs might easily adopt a code of institutions which would go by the name of their Chara*n*as. In the Chara*n*a-

* Indische Studien, i. p. 160 ff.

† Pâ*n*ini, iv. 2, 46.

vyûha, a work ascribed to *S*aunaka, which treats of these schools, there are enumerated five *S*âkhâs of the *R*ig-veda; and forty-two or in one recension forty-four out of eighty-six are mentioned of the Yajur-veda. Twelve out of a thousand are said to have once existed of the Sâman; and of the Atharva-veda only nine.* But only a very few of these editions have come down to us.

The Atharva*n*arahasya, a modern treatise on the Atharva-veda, attributing the same number of *S*âkhâs to the Sâma-veda and the Atharva-veda, speaks of twenty-one of the *R*ig-veda, and a hundred of the Yajur-veda. But of all these *S*âkhâs the *R*ig-veda is now extant only in one; the Yajus in three, and we may say in four; the Sâman perhaps in two; and the Atharvan in one. The only recension in which the Sa*m*hitâ of the *R*ig-veda is found, is that of the *S*âkala school. The text of the Black Yajus is extant in the recensions of the two schools, that of A'pastamba, and that of the Kâ*t*haka which belongs to the Charakas; and the White Yajus exists in the recensions of the Mâdhya*m*dina and the Kâ*n*va schools. The Sa*m*hita of the Sâman is preserved in the two recensions: in that of the Râ*n*âyanîyas, and probably also that of the Kauthumas. The text of the Atharvan is preserved only in the *S*aunaka school. Each *S*âkhâ claimed the possession of the only true and genuine Veda. The discrepancies between these *S*âkhâs, however, consisted chiefly in numerous variations of their arrangement of the sacred scriptures and in their subsequent accretions or total omissions of texts.

* Weber's Indische Studien, xiii. pp. 430ff.

Although *S*âkhâ and Chara*n*a were sometimes used synonymously, yet *S*âkhâ properly applies to the traditional text followed as in the phrase *sâkhâm adhîte*; and Chara*n*a an ideal succession of teachers and pupils. We should then understand by a *S*âkhâ a traditional recension of any of the Vedas, handed down by different Chara*n*as, or different schools or sects, which strictly adhered to their own traditional text and interpretation. The Brahmans themselves were fully aware of this difference between a *S*âkhâ and a Chara*n*a. And it is highly probable that new Chara*n*as on sacred texts peculiar to them, were established in case of gross or slight discrepancies in the text of the hymns, as well as divergences in the Brâhma*n*as, as a *S*âkhâ always consisted of a Sa*m*hitâ and a Brâhma*n*a.

A Parishad means an assembly or a settlement of Brahmans associated for the study of the Vedas;* and the Pârshada might be the title of any book belonging to a Parishad. The law books lay down the number, age, and qualifications of the Brahmans who must have composed such an assembly to give decisive opinions on all subjects they would be referred to. The members of the same Chara*n*a might become fellows of different Parishads and *vice versâ.* The real ancestors of the Brahmans are eight in number; and eight gotras are again divided into forty-nine different gotras, and these constitute a still larger number of families. Gotras were confined to Brahmans as well as to Kshattriyas, and Vai*s*yas; and they depended on a community of blood corresponding to families. Cha-

* Vrihadâra*n*yaka, vi. 2.

ra*n*as existed among the priestly caste only; and they depended on the community of the sacred texts, and as such they were merely ideal fellowships. All the Brahman families that keep and preserve sacred or sacrificial fire claim a descent from the seven *R*ishis.* A Brahman is bound by law to know to which of the forty-nine gotras his own family belongs; and in consecrating his own fire he must invoke the ancestors who founded the gotra to which he belongs. Such names as *gotra*, *varga*, *paksha*, and *gana* are all used in one and the same sense. And these genealogies represent something real, and have an historical value.

From the Brâhma*n*as sprung those mystical and theosophical writings, the A'ra*n*yakas and the Upanishads. By the word A'ra*n*yaka Pâ*n*ini understands a forester.† If the theosophical works called the A'ra*n*yakas were extant during his time, he would have recognized them as a portion of the sacred literature. The A'ra*n*yakas are so called, according to Sâya*n*a, because they were read in the forest, as if they were the text books of the anchorites, whose devotions were purely spiritual.‡ Of the A'ra*n*yakas there are four extant, the V*r*ihad, the Taittirîya, the Aitareya, and the Kaushîtaki. These, no doubt, belong to a class of Sanskrit writings, the history of which has not yet been properly investigated. Their style is full of strange solecisms.§ The A'ra*n*yakas contain the quintes-

* Bh*r*igu, Angiras, Visvâmitra, Vasish*t*ha, Kasyapa, Atri and Agasti.

† अरण्यान् मनुष्ये । iv, 2, 129.

‡ Goldstücker's Pâ*n*ini, p. 129; Weber's Indische Studien, v. p. 149.

§ Cowell's Kaushîtaki-Upanishad, p. viii.

sence of the Vedas and they only treat of the science of Brahma. The A'ranyakas, as an enlargement upon the Brâhmanas, presuppose their existence. They are anterior to the Sûtras, and likewise they are posterior to the Brâhmanas to which they form a kind of appendix.

The A'ranyakas discuss the obscure points of religion and philosophy, the nature of God, the creation of the world, and the relation of man to God and subjects of a like nature. The names of the authors are unknown to us, because their authorship was disclaimed on the ground that the productions would lose all their divine authority; and also because those productions are mere compilations from other works. However they exhibit the very dawn of thought; and the problems discussed in them are not in themselves modern; but still modes of modern thought are not altogether wanting in them. And they abound also in passages which are unequalled in any language, for grandeur, simplicity and boldness.

The original Upanishads, or the Mysteries of Theosophy, had their place in the A'ranyakas and the Brâhmanas. The most important of them are full of theosophy and philosophy. Max Müller has surmised that the word Upanishad "meant originally the act of sitting down near a teacher, of submissively listening to him," whence it came to mean "implicit faith, and at last truth or divine revelation."* It may even be supposed with some reason that these works derived their names from the mysteriousness of the doctrines contained in them; and perhaps also from the mystical and obscure manner in which

* Müller's History of Ancient Sanskrit Literature, p. 319.

they propound them. It is very probable that in the time of Pâ*n*ini, the works bearing the name of Upanishads were not in existence.* The Upanishads are mere compilations from other works; and the names of the authors of the principal ones are unknown. They are commonly in the form of dialogue; and in the main written in prose with occasional fragments of verse, but sometimes they are all in verse. The oldest among them may date as far back as the sixth century B. C. They are the V*r*ihadâra*n*yaka, the Aitareya, the Chhândogya, the Taittirîya, the Isa, the Kena, the Prasna, the Ka*t*ha, the Mu*nd*aka and the Mâ*nd*ûkya. The ordinary enumeration of them exceeds a hundred; but most of them are apocryphal. All the fifty-one were translated into Latin and published by Anquetil Duperron in 1801, under the title of "Oupnekhat" or "Theosophia Indica." His translations were mostly from a Persian version prepared by the orders of Dara Shukoh. The various systems of Hindu philosophy have their basis in the Upanishads, though quite antagonistic in their character. Most of the modern Upanishads are the works of Gau*d*apâda, *S*ankara, and other philosophers. Founders of new sects composed numerous other Upanishads of their own as the ancient ones did not suit their purpose.† The original Upanishads must ever occupy a prominent place in the sacred literature of the Indo-Aryans. The theological and philosophical

* Goldstücker's Pâ*n*ini, p. 141.

† Ward's View of the History, Literature and Mythology of the Hindus, ii. p. 61.

speculations they contain are sublime productions of the human mind. They are the most ancient monuments of philosophical conceptions, and as such they are far more advanced both in the depth and loftiness of their ideas and opinions than any of the Greek schools prior to Socrates, except that of Elea. They contributed much towards the formation of the civil and domestic polity, and directed the whole tone of moral ordinances. They are considered with some show of reason as the highest authorities on which the various systems of philosophy are said to rest. The Vedânta philosopher seeks some warranty for his faith in the Veda; and the Sânkhya, the Vaiseshika, the Nyâya and the Yoga philosophers profess to find in the Upanishads some authority for their opinions though there is no ground of harmony among them; the chief object of the Upanishads being to unfold the darkest points of philosophy and religion, to discuss the creation of the world, to descant on the nature of God, and to elucidate the relation of man to God and the like. There is however not to be found any systematic uniformity in the Upanishads; and the philosophy contained in them is as sublime as it is in some places puerile. Indeed, they have with some exceptions clearly distinguished the principle of spiritual existence; and have successfully made the distinction between concrete existence and abstract being. But in fact the authors of them are merely poets rather than true philosophers, who throw out rhapsodies which are altogether unconnected and often contradictory, and seem to have no thought or even care of bringing into agreement to-day's feelings with those of yesterday or of tomorrow.* They shadow forth the later Vedânta as the oracular denunciations of Herakleitos shadow forth the complete developed system of the Platonic philosophy. The reader of the Upanishads finds no difficulty in recognising familiar ideas in the rigid speculations of Plato as well as of Empedocles or Pythagoras, in the Neo-platonism of the Alexandrian school, as well as in the philosophy of the Gnostics. The Upanishads contain mythological as well as theosophical elements ; and they exhibit a freedom of thought which was in fact the beginning of Hindû philosophy. And the key-note of the old Upanishads is "Know thyself." The Upanishads, from the beginning to the end, consist of texts which propound that God is the one spirit, which is the substance of the universe ; that the creation is nothing else than a multiplication and development of Himself ; and that the universe is to Him what the butter is to the milk. They inculcate pantheism of one kind or another ; but their pantheism is, beyond doubt, of a very spiritual kind. Thet heory of no two of them can be regarded precisely the same. Some of them abound in speculations, much after the fashion of development philosophers, on the physical primeval element of the universe ; and whatever is, on the impulse of the moment accepted as a first principle, is announced to be Brahma or God. The great teachers of this *parâ*, or superior knowledge, were Kshattriyas, and Brahmans are merely represented as becoming pupils of the great Kshattriya kings. The Kshattriya mind first carried on these bold speculations ; and we can scarcely

* Banerjea's Dialogues on Hindu Philosophy, pp. 14, 42 ff.

avoid this conclusion when we add to this the remarkable fact that the Gâyatrî itself, the most sacred prayer of the Brahmans, is a hymn by an author, not a Brahman but a Kshattriya.* The Upanishads abound in descriptions not merely of carnal observances; but also of obscenities still worse and grosser than Jayadeva's battles of love.

The B*r*ihadâra*n*yaka constitutes the last five prapâ*t*hakas of the fourteenth book of the *S*atapatha-Brâhma*n*a in the Mâdhya*m*dina-*s*âkhâ. The Upanishad properly so called is divided into six chapters, and each chapter is again subdivided into different brâhma*n*as. It wears a purely speculative and legendary character; and deals with the doctrine of the transmigration of souls. The Taittirîya-A'ra*n*yaka includes ten prapâ*t*hakas, of which the last four are styled the Upanishad, and the first six are properly called the A'ra*n*yaka. It is throughout ritualistic, and represents the latest period of Vaidik ideas. The sixth chapter of the A'ra*n*yaka gives in detail the whole of the funeral ceremonies required to be observed at burials. The Taittirîya-Upanishad is a part of the Taittirîyâra*n*yaka of the Black Yajus. It is divided into three chapters, the *S*ikshâ-vallî, the Brahmânanda-vallî, and the Bh*r*igu-vallî. We trace in it the germ of the Vedânta system. The Taittirîyâra*n*yaka is older than the B*r*ihadâra*n*yaka. It shows a strange medley of post-Vaidik ideas and names. The Aitareyâra*n*yaka consists of five books and forms a work by itself; the second and third books of which form the Bahv*r*icha-Upanishad. The first book is arranged in five chapters; the second in seven; the third in two; the fourth in one;

* Visvâmitra.

and the fifth in three. These chapters again are sub-divided into a number of kha*n*das. With reference to its subjects the Aitareya may be divided into two parts, the first liturgical, and the second philosophical. This A'ra*n*yaka is not the work of the same individual; and the first three books are said to be written under divine inspiration, and the rest by human authors. The Aitareya is more speculative and mystical than legendary or practical. There is another A'ra*n*yaka called the Kaushîtaki-A'ra*n*yaka, which is divided into three books of which the third constitutes the Kaushîtaki-Upanishad. This A'ra*n*yaka treats more of ritual than of speculation. The Kaushîtaki-Upanishad consists of four chapters; and there is no doubt that it is contemporaneous with the B*r*ihadâra*n*yaka of the White Yajus.* There are no A'ra*n*yakas for the Sâma-veda, nor for the Atharva-veda. The A'ra*n*yakas derive their authority from *S*ruti. Sâya*n*a states that the Taittirîya-Upanishad comprises three parts, and they go by the names of Sâ*m*hitî, Yâjnikî, and Vârunî; of these the last is the most important, because it teaches the knowledge of the Divine Self. The Aitareya is included in the second A'ra*n*yaka of the Aitareya-Brâhma*n*a. It contains three chapters. The Taittirîya and Aitareya resemble each other in a great measure. The *S*vetâ*s*vatara is comparatively modern. In fact, it does not belong to the series of the more ancient Upanishads. It was composed after the publication of the Vedânta and Sânkhya; and is a compound of the Vedânta pantheism and the Sânkhya duality. The Vâjasaneyi-Upanishad is very short. It is composed of only eighteen

* Weber's History of Indian Literature, p. 51.

srutis; and forms an index to the Vâjasaneyi-Sa*m*hitâ. The Talavakâra, or Kena-Upanishad, which is one of the shortest and the most philosophical treatises of this kind, puts in clearer language, perhaps, than any other Upanishad, the doctrine that the true knowledge of the Supreme Spirit consists in the consciousness which man acquires of his complete inability to understand him, since the human mind being capable only of comprehending finite objects, cannot have a knowledge of what is infinite. The Kena is included in both the Atharvan and the Sâman. The Ka*t*ha has always been considered as one of the best Upanishads; and it must be admitted, that in point of elevation of thought, depth of expression, beauty of its imagery, and ingenuous fervour, few stand equal to it. It consists of two adhyâyas, each of which contains three vallîs. The first part is quite independent. But the second is composed almost entirely of Vaidik quotations, which prove more in detail the doctrine enunciated in the first. It is on this account that both the parts are with some reason taken as two distinct Upanishads. There can be no doubt as to the second part being later than the first; and this is clear from several other, particularly linguistic, reasons. But Dr. Weber is of opinion that the Ka*t*ha originally closed with the third vallî.* This Upanishad treats, first, of the highest object of man; second, the First Cause of the world and his attributes; third, the connexion of this Cause with the world. These questions are mooted in the different chapters in a manner which is quite peculiar to the Upanishads

* Weber's Indische Studien, ii. pp. 197-200 ff.

in general. The stand-point of the Ka*th*a is, however, on the whole that of the scholastic doctrines of the Vedânta philosophy. We cannot give the same credit to the philosophy as to the form of the Ka*th*a. There is scarcely any link connecting the thoughts, so that they rather show that it is plainly a compilation than the production of an original and devout thinker. According to the Ka*th*a, the knowledge of Brahma hangs upon a process of thinking, *i. e.* it is derived from philosophy, and not from revelation. The Prasna, one of the Upanishads of the Atharva-veda, is divided into six chapters, each of which attempts to solve a distinct question. From the first question we arrive at the knowledge of the relation that exists between Prajâpati and the creatures, the period of creation, and the manner in which Prajâpati is to be worshipped. The description is altogether mythological and symbolical, and does not show any well-defined thought. The second shews his relation to the individual bodies. From the third question we should understand that life, when produced from the soul, is divided into the five vital airs, by whose regular actions the functions of the body are sustained. The remaining part of this question furnishes us with a specimen of the anatomical and physiological knowledge of the author; and a bold attempt to apply the functions observed in the microcosm of the human body to the macrocosm of the world. The fourth question is free from mythological embellishments, and gives the substance of the doctrines of the entire Upanishad.

The Mu*nd*aka-Upanishad contains three mu*nd*akas; each of which is sub-divided into two kha*nd*as. There are two sciences, according to the first mun*d*aka, the *aparâ* and the *parâ*. The former is founded on the four Vedas and the six Vedângas ; the latter refers to Brahma, that Being who is incomprehensible to the organs of action and intellect, and is without qualities. We find mention of the Vedânta and Yoga in this Upanishad. "It would almost be a contradiction in terms, to say that the Mun*d*aka is a section of the Atharva-veda, which it condemns, along with the others, as inferior science. And if it must be referred to a post-Vaidik age, it would be difficult to affirm that it was composed before the age of Buddha."* The identity between the Ka*t*ha, Pra*s*na and Mun*d*aka appears not merely in the mode of explanation, but also in the images and in entire passages. More particularly is this the case between the Mun*d*aka and Ka*t*ha than between the Mun*d*aka and Pra*s*na Upanishads. Which of these Upanishads was the original, or what relation they bear to other sources, can hardly be determined. This much, however, may be said, that the Pra*s*na bears every mark of compilation. The Mân*d*ûkya has only twelve *slokas*. In these *slokas* the meaning of the mystical syllable *Om* is unravelled. This Upanishad is taken from various sources. From it, the contents having been stripped of their abstruse phraseology, we are to understand that Brahma comprehends all things, both objects of perception and those that are beyond the reach of perception. Brahma has four modes of existence, the waking state, the state of dreaming, the state of profound sleep, and a fourth state quite different from any of the former ; this state is indes-

* Banerjea's Dialogues.

cribable, in which all manifestations cease, it is blissful and without duality. The Mândûkya is one of the latest among the Upanishads which show the infinite spirit in its primitive notion, wholly uninfluenced by sectarian views. The order, in which the state of Brahma's existence is described, exhibits, on the whole, a very profound mode of thought. The Chhândogya-Upanishad consists of eight chapters. It is more modern than the Brihadâranyaka, which probably belongs to the eastern part of Hindustan.* In the Chhândogyopanishad a number of most curious modes of *upâsanâs* are prescribed. One of these devotions is so grossly obscene and filthy that we must refrain from translating or reproducing it here. The Bahvrichas placed A'tman or the Self at the beginning of all things. The Taittirîyakas speak of Brahma as true, omniscient and infinite. Calling Brahma as neuter, they give proofs of their having been impressed with the idea of a Power. It was decidedly an era in the history of the human intellect when the apparent identity of the Self in the masculine, and Brahma in the neuter, was for the first time clearly established. The Chhandogas speak of a *Sat*, or a Being who has the tendency to be many. The A'tharvanikas speak of the Creator as *Akshara*; and it is very uncertain whether they used this word to mean Element or the Indestructible. The term used by the Vâjasaneyins is *Avyâkrita*, or the Undeveloped. The Upanishads are the principal parts of the Vedas. Of all the Vaidik works, they were the last composed.

The Mantras, the Brâhmanas, the A'ranyakas, and the

* Weber's History of Indian Literature, p. 70.

Upanishads are designated under the term of *S*ruti; while the term Sm*r*iti includes the Vedângas, the Sûtras, either *S*rauta or G*r*ihya, &c. *S*ruti means revelation, and Sm*r*iti recollection. The Mantras are either metrical hymns or prose forms of prayer, in which the praises of the gods are celebrated, and their blessing is invoked. The *R*ik and the Sâman consist of hymns of the former description. The Brâhma*n*as arose out of the hymns, and so stand next to them. They embrace liturgical regulations regarding the ceremonial employment of the hymns, and the celebration of various rites and sacrifices; and include also such treatises as the A'ra*n*yakas and the Upanishads. The A'ra*n*yakas and Upanishads are theological treatises, which bear the same character as do some of the older portions of the Brâhma*n*as. They give very distinct indications of spiritual aspirations, and also of ideas of a speculative and mystical character such as we find in the hymns, and in the earlier portions of the Brâhma*n*as; but only with this exception that in those treatises they have been further matured as they developed in the minds of subsequent generations of sages. The distinction between *S*ruti and Sm*r*iti had been established by the Brahmans prior to the rise of Buddhism, or prior to the time when the style of the Sûtras gained admittance into Indian literature. This difference, in fact, occurs in the Brâhma*n*as.* The term Sm*r*iti is also met with in the Taittirîyâra*n*yaka,† though it is used there in the sense of *S*ruti. That Sm*r*iti has no claim to an independent authority, but derives its

* Aitareya-Brâhma*n*a, vii. 9.

† Taittirîyâra*n*yaka, i. 1, 2.

sanction from its relation to *S*ruti, is to be understood by its very name which means tradition. In the Sûtras the distinction is clearly made between *S*ruti and Sm*r*iti. We also find the same distinction in the Anupada-Sûtra.* And in the Nidâna-Sûtra ancient tradition is also mentioned under the name of Sm*r*iti.†

* Anupada-Sûtra, ii. 4.

† Nidâna-Sûtra, ii. 1.

CHAPTER V.

The Peculiarities of the Sûtras—the Vedângas—the Origin and General Character of the Prâtisâkhyas—the Anukramanîs—the Parisishtas—the Origin of Buddhism—the Knowledge of Writing in ancient India.

THE Sûtra is the technical name given to aphoristic rules, and also to those works which consist of such rules. The Sûtras, upon the whole, rest, though not entirely, upon the Brâhmanas. The importance of the term, however, may be conceived from the fact, that the groundworks of the whole ritual, grammatical, metrical, and philosophical literature of India are indited in the aphoristic style, which exhibits one of the peculiarities of Indian authorship. Though there is no clear evidence as to the cause which gave birth to this peculiarity in Sanskrit composition; the method of instruction followed in ancient India renders it probable that these Sûtras were so composed as to facilitate the studies of pupils who had to learn simply by heart. But it is also equally probable that this method of schooling itself gained ground owing to the want of suitable materials for writing purposes, and in consequence of the expediency of economising those materials so far as could be possible. Thus great brevity and a rigid economy of words was practised. The Sûtra works are all brief, systematic, and enigmatical. Every doctrine thus propounded in them is so strained and twisted in every possible manner that it is almost reduced to mere algebraic symbols. The most obscure brevity is the principal object which guided the authors of the Sûtra works. "Even the bare simplicity of the design vanishes in the perplexity of the structure." Owing to curtness and elliptical obscurity these Sûtras are almost unintelligible. In fact, to acquire mastery over the Sûtra works is next to impossible, without the help of the key which is found in separate Sûtras called Paribhâshâ. Notwithstanding this key the student also must be in possession of the laws of the so-called Anuvritti and Nirvritti. They are certainly one of the most curious sorts of literary composition that the human mind has ever produced; and if altogether worthless in an artistic point of view, it is remarkable that the Indo-Aryans should have fabricated this most difficult form, and adopted it as the most convenient vehicle of expression of every branch of learning.

The elaborate and overstrained conciseness of the Sûtras renders them in a high degree obscure and ambiguous. Notwithstanding the key to their interpretations, there are to be found many seeming contradictions. The Sûtras bewilder even a scholar, and puzzle him at the very threshold in the obscure labyrinth of symbols and abbreviations. The Sûtra works contain the quintessence of all the knowledge which was then floating about in the Parishads, and which the Brahmans themselves had accumulated during many centuries of study and reflection. The cut and dry style of the Sûtra is so peculiar to India that it allows of no comparison with the style of composition of other countries in the early times when they were composed.

We have to search for the Vedânga doctrines in all their originality and authenticity in the Brâhma*n*as and the Sûtras; and not in those barren tracts which are now known by the name of Vedângas. The Vedângas are not parts of the Vedas themselves, but supplementary to them; and in the form in which we now possess them, are not wholly genuine; and in fact, are of little importance. They are, however, auxiliary books for understanding the Vedas. All those works were written with an object of their being practical; and they exhibit quite a novel phase in the literature of the ancient Indians. Their authors were not inspired, and the style which they employed to subserve their purpose, was business-like on the whole. Manu calls them Pravachanas,* a title which is usually applied to the Brâhma*n*as. We find the earliest mention of the six Vedângas in one of the Brâhma*n*as of the Sâman.† Yâska (Nir. i. 20) only quotes the Vedângas; but he does not give the title of any of them. The number of the six Vedângas is given in the Chara*n*avyûha, in Manu (iii. 185) and also in the Chhândogyopanishad. The Mu*nd*akopanishad also gives us the entire number of the Vedângas.

* Manu, iii. 184.

† Sha*d*vinsa-Brâhma*n*a, iv. 7.

A clear statement as to the rational character of the Vedângas is given in the Brihadâranyaka and in its commentary.

The first Vedânga is called *S*ikshâ which, according to Sâyana, who lived in the 14th century A. D.,* comprises rules regarding letters, accents, quantity, organs, enumeration, delivery, and euphonic combinations. This little treatise is ascribed to Pânini; and it is possible that we may not find it to be an original Vedânga work. Pânini's *S*ikshâ consists in one recension of thirty-five, and in another of fifty-nine verses. We have another tract on *S*ikshâ, called the Mândûkî-*S*ikshâ, which is probably a later production of the Sûtra period; but it is of great importance as it bears the name of a certain Charana of the *R*ig-veda, the Mândûkâyana. The rules on *S*ikshâ had formerly a place in the seventh book of the Taittirîyâranyaka; and Sâyana also takes the same view in his commentary on the Sâmhitî-Upanishad. In fact, this book is called the *S*ikshâ chapter; and it is more than doubtful whether it was ever considered as such.† It is also supposed that those rules lost this place by the appearance of the Prâtisâkhyas. But nothing is found in the Pushpa-Sûtra of Gobhila to prove this. The *S*ikshâs are older than the Prâtisâkhyas. Their doctrines, no doubt, were incorporated and highly developed in the latter.

The second is called Chhandas which treats of metre. But the *S*âkala Prâtisâkhya contains some chapters on

* Wilson's *R*ig-veda, i. p. xlviii; Müller's Sanskrit Researches, p. 187.

† Indian Antiquary, v. pp. 141 ff; 193 ff.

metre, which are far more valuable than this utterly unimportant work known by the name of Chhandas. The work of Pingalanâga on Chhandas, which is frequently quoted under the title of Vedânga, is not of great antiquity; and it becomes very doubtful whether it is an original Vedânga work.* Some suppose Pingala was the same as Patanjali, the author of the Mahâbhâshya.† But the identity of Pingala and Patanjali is far from being probable.' It is not surprising that Pingala does not confine himself exclusively to the metres of Sanskrit. He also gives rules bearing on the metres of Prâk*r*ita; and even Kâtyâyana-vararuchi, the author of the Vârttikas on Pâ*n*ini, the great Father of Sanskrit Grammar, is said to have written a Prâk*r*ita grammar. It must be admitted that the treatise of Pingala on Chhandas was one of the last books that were included in the Sûtra period. Prof. Wilson supposes it to be scarcely regarded as belonging to this period. But on no ground can we exclude it from this period altogether. Pingala is quoted as an authority on metre in the Pari*s*ish*t*as. We learn from Sha*d*guru*s*ishya that Pingala was the younger brother, or at least the descendant of Pâ*n*ini. And according to some Pingala may be as old as the second century B. C.

The third is called Vyâkara*n*a. The Indo-Aryans cultivated the science of grammar from the earliest times. Eight different schools of grammar prevailed in India. Pâ*n*ini's system undoubtedly superseded all other systems. Of all these schools of grammar the Aindra was the

* Weber's History of Indian Literature, p. 66.

† Colebrooke's Essays, ii. p. 63.

oldest; and the treatises of that school are actually quoted by Pâ*n*ini.* Pâ*n*ini is the only representative of this Vedânga; and his grammar consists of eight adhyâyas or books, each adhyâya comprising four pâdas or chapters, and each pâda a number of sûtras or aphoristic rules. The latter amount on the whole to 3996 sûtras composed with the symbolic brevity of the most concise *memoria technica*; but three or four of them did not originally belong to the work. The sûtras are all made up of the driest technicalities; and their arrangement, on the whole, is based on the principle of tracing linguistic phenomena. In a general manner, Pâ*n*ini's grammar may be called a natural history of the Sanskrit language. He records such phenomena of the language as are exceedingly interesting and valuable from a grammatical point of view. Words which he has treated of are also of historical and antiquarian interest. He also gives very useful information about the ancient geography of India. His grammar is built, no doubt, on the perfect phonetic system of which he was not altogether the inventor.† The source of Pâ*n*ini's purely grammatical doctrines must be sought for elsewhere; and it is sufficiently evident that he quotes various grammarians who had preceded him. To fix the age in which Pâ*n*ini lived, is a task we are incapable of performing; as many of the Indian authors shine, to use the words of a well-known Sanskrit scholar, like fixed stars in India's literary firmament, but no telescope can discover any appreciable dia-

* Burnell's Aindra Grammarians, p. 2.

† Weber's History of Indian Literature, p. 216.

meter. However it must be of some interest to know whether that Patriarch of Sanskrit Philology is likely to have lived before or after the death of Buddha. According to the views expressed by Prof. Goldstücker it is probable that Pânini lived before Buddha, the founder of the Buddhist religion, whose death took place about 543 B. C.; but that a more definite date of the great Grammarian can hardly be obtained in the present condition of Sanskrit philology. Müller holds Pânini to be anterior to Yâska, but Yâska is noticed by Pânini himself;* and there can be no doubt that Pânini was posterior to Yâska. Pânini was a native of Salâtura, situated in the Gandhâra country north-west of Attock on the Indus. Whence he is also called Sâlâturîya. His mother was called Dâkshi. He was a descendant of Panin, and grandson of Devala. He belonged, therefore, to the north-western or western school.

The Mahâbhâshya by Patanjali is not a full commentary of Pânini, but with some exceptions, only a commentary on the Vârttikas or critical remarks of Kâtyâyana on Pânini; and so it is rather a controversial manual. From circumstantial evidence Prof. Goldstücker has proved that Patanjali wrote his Mahâbhâshya between 140 and 120 B. C.† Kâtyâyana, the critic of the great Grammarian was most likely the same with the Kâtyâyana who wrote the grammatical treatise called the Prâtisâkhya of the White Yajus. Goldstücker has further shown that

* Pânini, ii. 4, 63 : यास्कादिभ्यो गोत्रे । See also Lassen's Indian Antiquities, i. pp. 864-866., ii. p. 476.

† Pânini : His Place in Sanskrit Literature, p. 235ff.

he could not have been the contemporary of Pâṇini as is generally supposed. He has also proved that this Kâtyâyana was the contemporary of Patanjali; and probably being the teacher of the latter, he must have lived in the middle of the second century before Christ.* Kâtyâyana completed and corrected Pâṇini's grammar; and his Vârttikas show a more wide and profound knowledge of Sanskrit than the work of Pâṇini himself. We obtain some information about Kâtyâyana from the Kathâsaritsâgara, the encyclopædia of legends, by Somadeva Bhatta of Kashmir. But after all we are to reject it as an episode in the story of a ghost. Somadeva composed it for the entertainment of the grand-mother of *S*rî Harshadevà, king of Kashmir, who ascended the throne of that country in 1059 and reigned, according to Abû'l-fazel, only 12 years; and consequently it must have been written between 1059 and 1071, or a few years earlier. The Kathâsaritsâgara is supposed by many to be the sheet-anchor of Indian chronology.

There are two other works on grammatical subjects: the Uṇṇâdi-Sûtras and the Phiṭ-Sûtras of Sântanâchârya. As to when Sântana's Phiṭ-Sûtras were composed we are perfectly in the dark. Pâṇini does not presuppose a knowledge of them; and the grammatical terms employed by Sântana are quite different from those adopted by Pâṇini. Although those Sûtras treat simply of accents, and accents such as are used in the Vaidik language; the subject of Sântana's work does not warrant us to suppose that he was

* Weber's Indische Studien, xiii. p, 297, ff.

anterior to Pâ*n*ini. "The U*n*âdi-Sûtras are rules for deriving, from the acknowledged verbal roots of the Sanskrit, a number of appellative nouns, by means of a species of suffixes, which, though nearly allied to the so-called *krits*, are not commonly used for the purposes of derivation." . . . "A peculiarity of all words derived by an u*n*âdi is, that, whether they be substantives or adjectives, they do not express a general or indefinite agent, but receive an individual signification, not necessarily resulting from the combination of the suffix with a verbal root."* The U*nn*âdi-Sûtras we now possess, are not in their original form. It was not the object of the author to give a complete list of all the u*nn*âdi words, but merely to collect the most important of them. In fact, these were originally intended for the Veda only, and subsequently enlarged by the addition of rules on the formation of non-Vaidik words. It is not known by whom the U*nn*âdi-Sûtras were first collected. Pâ*n*ini frequently refers in his Sûtras to a list of affixes or u*nn*âdis, but not to the U*nn*âdi-Sûtras.† It is, therefore, probable that those affixes must have existed before his time.‡ By some the U*nn*âdi-Sûtras are ascribed to *S*âka*t*âyana, an ancient grammarian anterior to Yâska, and a *S*ûdra and follower of Buddha. But a very interesting passage in Viralâ's Rupamâlâ distinctly ascribes the authorship of the U*nn*âdi-Sûtras to Vararuchi who is no other than Kâtyâyana.¶

* Aufrecht's U*n*âdi-Sûtras, p. v.

† Pâ*n*ini, iii. 3, 1 ; iii. 4, 75.

‡ Müller's History of Ancient Sanskrit Literature, p. 151.

¶ Ibid. p. 240.

The fourth Vedânga is the Nirukta of Yâska, the oldest glossator on the Veda. The Nirukta is a sort of commentary on the Nigha*nt*us ; and it is found frequently to refer to the Brâhma*n*as, and bring forward various legends such as those about Devâpi (xi. 10) and Vi*s*vâmitra (ii. 24). The Nirukta is older than Pâ*n*ini. Yâska also furnishes us with the names of no less than seventeen interpreters who had preceded him ;* but their explanations of the Veda generally conflict with one another. The Nigha*nt*us comprise a vocabulary of synonymous, obsolete, and obscure Vaidik terms. The Nigha*nt*us and Nirukta are closely connected ; the former is older than the latter. Yâska ascribes the Nigha*nt*us to an ancient tradition. If the Nirukta belongs to Yâska, the Nigha*nt*us also could not have been written by him. However to the Nirukta we are inclined to attribute a very high antiquity ; it belongs to the oldest part of Sanskrit literature excepting the Vaidik writings, and to an already far advanced period of grammar and interpretation.

Yâska prefixed the Nigha*nt*us to his own work, the Nirukta, in which he throws light on the obscure passages of the Vedas. The Nirukta consists of three parts. The first part or the Naigha*nt*uka comprises a collection of synonymous words, the second or Naigama a collection of words peculiar to the Vedas, and the third or Daivata words relating to deities and sacrifices. In this Vedânga we find the first fundamental notions of grammar. It is obvious that when this work of Yâska was composed,

* Roth's Illustrations, pp. 221f. ; see also Weber's History of Indian Literature, p. 26.

and even at a much earlier period, the sense of most of the Vaidik words had become completely obscure. This clearly appears from the fact of such works as the Nighantus and Nirukta being written at all. The Nirukta together with the Prâtisâkhyas and the grammar of Pânini supplies the most important information on the growth of grammatical science in India. Yâska is wholly unacquainted with such algebraical symbols as are contained in Pânini. The introduction to the Nirukta, which supplies us with a full sketch of a grammatical and exegetical system, gives the views of Yâska and his predecessors; and in this manner we are able to establish a complete comparison of these older grammarians with Pânini.

The fifth is the Kalpa or the Ceremonial. The Brâhmanas are the sources of the Vaidik ritual, which became completely developed and systematized in the ritual works called the Kalpa-Sûtras. The composition of the Kalpa-Sûtras is in some respects an important event in the Vaidik history. Though they do not claim to be Smritis, yet they are enumerated amongst the Svâdhyâyas. The Kalpa-Sûtras must have been drawn up for the easy reference of the priests, who would otherwise have to grope in the dark through the liturgical Samhitâs and Brâhmanas for the *disjecta membra* of the sacrificial and other rites. Thus we possess Kalpa-Sûtras connected with the Rig-veda by A'svalâyana, Sânkhâyana and Saunaka; with the Sâma-veda by Masaka, Lâtyâyana, Gobhila, Drâhyâyana, and a Sûtra called Anupada-Sûtra; with the Black Yajur-veda by A'pastamba, Baudhâyana, Satyâshâdha-Hiranyakesin, Mânava, Bhâradvâja, etc.; with the

White Yajur-veda by Kâtyâyana; and with the Atharva-veda by Kusika. There is another Kalpa work belonging to the Atharva-veda, which is called the Vaitâna-Sûtra; and which cannot claim a very remote antiquity. The Vaitâna-Sûtra presupposes the existence of the Kausika-Sûtra. Kâtyâyana also takes notice of this Sûtra work. It bears the same relation to the Gopatha-Brâhmana as does the A'svalâyana *S*rauta-Sûtra to the Aitareya-Brâhma*n*a.* Though it is a *S*rauta-Sûtra of the Atharvan it was composed under the influence of the Yajus. It does not contain at all magical hymns and conjurations; but it contains much interesting matter which we do not find in other ritual works.† The Kalpa-Sûtras are divided into three classes, such as *S*rauta, G*r*ihya, and Sâmayâchârika: the first prescribes the especial Vaidik ceremonials, such as those which are to be celebrated on the days of new and full moon. The rites according to the *S*rauta-Sûtras can be performed by rich people and no others; and have therefore been made obligatory only under certain restrictions. The second enjoins the domestic rites to be performed at various stages of life from birth to death. The G*r*ihya-Sûtras give general rules which are to be observed at marriages, at the birth of a child, on the day of naming the child, at the tonsure and investiture of a boy, and at the time of and after the death of a person. Indeed, the G*r*ihya-Sûtras contain all the rules bearing on those principal and purificatory ceremonies which are included under the

* Haug's Aitareya-Brâhma*n*a i. p. 8; see also Weber's History of Indian Literature, p. 57.

† Garbe's Vaitâna-Sûtra, pp. v.-viii; see also Weber's Indische Studien, x. p. 176; and Roth's Atharva-veda in Kashmir, p. 22.

general name of *samskâras** or certain sacramental rites. The rites and ceremonies according to the Grihya are called Pâkayajna or sacrifices with food. A Pâkayajna consists in a piece of wood being placed in the fire in a hearth, oblations made to the gods, and gifts bestowed on the Brahmans. The third regulates the daily observances of the twice born. The rules of the Sâmayâchârika-Sûtras are based rather on secular than sacred authority. They describe the duties of a student as a Brahmachârin or catechumen in the house of his preceptor. They regulate the proper diet of a Brahman. They prescribe what food is allowable and what not; what days should be allotted for fasting; and what penances ought to be performed for not observing duty. They decide, in a great measure, the duties and rights of kings and magistrates, the civil rights of the people at large, and even rules of social politeness. Of the Grihya-Sûtras of the Rig-veda, we have those by Sânkhâyana and A'svalâyana; a Grihya-Sûtra of the Sâma-veda is that of Gobhila; of the Black Yajur-veda we possess the Baudhâyana; and of the White Yajur-veda, the Pâraskara Grihya-Sûtras. The Drâhyâyana belongs to the school of the Rânâyanîyas. It differs but slightly from the Lâtyâyana, and treats, on the whole, of the same identical matter. The Lâtyâyana belongs to the school of the Kauthumas. The first seven prapâthakas of the Lâtyâyana-Sûtras contain the injunctions applicable to all the Soma sacrifices; the 8th and part of the 9th prapâthaka treat of the *ekâhas*; the remainder of the 9th of the *ahînas*; and the 10th of the *sattras* or sessions.

* Cf. Wilson's Dictionary, s. v.

The Kalpa-Sûtras mark a new period in the literary and religious history of India; and they contributed, no doubt, to the total extinction of the numerous Brâhmanas. From a comparison of the Brâhmanas with the Kalpa books it appears that the difference between them is of great importance. They are found to treat in the most elaborate manner of the entire system of divine worship, each in a quite different way. The Kalpa books establish the whole course of the rites of worship. They direct which of the priests have to take part at each of the stages of the sacred rites, what hymns are to be recited, and further define the time and place for the celebration of those rites. But the object of a Brâhmana is very different from the Kalpa works; its subject being the "brahma," the sacred element in the rite; from which we are to draw the most valuable information regarding the early conceptions on divine matters.* At any rate, the introduction of a Kalpa-Sûtra was the introduction of a new book of liturgy. The *S*rauta and G*r*ihya-Sûtras are of much greater value than the Sâmayâchârika. The G*r*ihya and Sâmayâchârika-Sûtras have generally been confounded; but the Brahmans draw a line of demarcation between the two, the G*r*ihya-ceremonies being performed by the married house-holder with no other purpose than for the benefit of his family. The *S*rauta-Sûtras mean the whole body of the Sûtras, the source of which can be traced to the *S*ruti or the literature of revelation, the Mantras and Brâhmanas; while the Smârta-

* Roth's Introduction to the Nirukta, p. xxiv, ff.

Sûtras can have claim to no such source. The main difference between the two lies not in their matter; but in the age and style of composition. The *S*rauta-Sûtras treat of the grand and public religious ceremonies, rites and sacrifices (Haviryajnas and Somayajnas). Both the G*r*ihya and Sâmayâchârika-Sûtras are included under the common title of Smârta-Sûtras in opposition to the *S*rauta-Sútras. The former derived their authority from the Sm*r*iti, and the latter from the *S*ruti. The Sâmayâchârika-Sútras are also called Dharma-Sútras, and they seem to have been the source of the Dharma-*s*âstras.* The Kalpa-Sútras are a complete system of ritualism, and give the whole method of the sacred ceremonial with great precision. It is not yet proved that the Kalpa-Sútras are a part of the Vedas; and in fact it is impossible to do. They were composed contemporaneously with Pâ*n*ini. We are here to observe once for all that there are ten Sútras of the Sâma-Veda; and these Sâma-Sútras do not all treat of the Kalpa or the Ceremonial. Some of them are more than mere lists, and their style approaches that of the Sútras. The ritual work called the Mânava-Kalpa-Sútras, which is connected with the Taittirîya-Sa*m*hitâ, sets forth or sanctions, more than the other Kalpa-Sútras, the dogmas and conclusions of the Mîmânsâ philosophers. This Kalpa-work is later than the Sútras of Baudhâyana and older than those of A'pastamba.† During the time of the composition of these Sútra works, the whole system of social organisation was developed, and

* Morley's Digest of Indian Cases, p. cxcvi.

† Goldstücker's Pâ*n*ini, p. 12.

the distinction of caste was fully established. On examining the Sûtra works and especially the Grihya-Sûtras we find that women had no right to the use of the Vedas. Yet, we learn from the same source that the husband in conjunction with his wife performed sacrifices and other rites. Women were allowed to repeat *mantras* at the time of sacrifices; and they were never scrupulously or entirely denied the knowledge of God.

The sixth and last of the Vedângas is Jyotisha. Works of astronomy were very scanty; and the only copy we now possess of it is comparatively modern, and its literature is also very meagre. The Jyotisha is a short tract embracing thirty-six verses, which are composed in a comparatively modern style. Its main object is to offer only such information about the heavenly bodies as were useful in fixing the days and hours of the Vaidik sacrifices and not to teach astronomy as a science.

The Prâtisâkhyas were designated Chara*n*as, because they were the property of the readers of certain Sâkhâs. They are really a sub-division of the Pârshada books. The Pârshada is another title often applied to the Prâtisâkhyas. The existing representatives of the Prâtisâkhyas, in all probability, were composed subsequent to the age of Pâ*n*ini;* and most of their rules are intended to supply the deficiencies in the Sûtras of that grammarian. The Prâtisâkhyas are nothing more than "theological and mystical dreams"; but they are not altogether destitute

* Goldstücker's Pâ*n*ini, p. 183 ff; Müller's *Rig*-veda Prâtisâkhya, Introduction; Weber's Indische Studien, xiii. p. 3 ff., and his History of Indian Literature, p. 24.

of exegetical or critical value. There is no doubt that they were written for practical purposes, and their style is free from cumbrous ornaments and unnecessary subtleties. Their object is to teach rather than to edify. A great number of authors are referred to in the Prâtiśâkhyas, and opinions with general precepts are found in them. Though we do not possess the works of the earlier authors, yet we may fairly assume that their favourite doctrines were treasured up originally in the shape of Prâtiśâkhyas. These writings contain rules on accent, Sandhi, on the permutation of sounds, the lengthening of the vowels in the Vedas, &c. The Kuladharmas could not be called Prâtiśâkhyas; but they might claim the title of Charaṇa or Pârshada.

There are Prâtiśâkhyas belonging to the *Ṛ*ig-veda, the Yajur-veda, and the Atharva-veda. The oldest among them is the *Ṛ*ig-veda-Prâtiśâkhya. But when the Taittirîya-Prâtiśâkhya or the Kâtyâyana-Prâtiśâkhya originated we cannot approximately say. The rules of the Prâtiśâkhyas were not merely a guide in the instructions of pupils who had to learn the texts of the Vedas by heart; but they were no doubt intended also for written literature. According to the representation of the Prâtiśâkhyas there are three modes of writing the Vedas, viz., the Saṁhitâ-pâṭha, the Pada-pâṭha, and the Krama-pâṭha. The Saṁhitâ-pâṭha means the mode of writing according to the rules of permutation; the Pada-pâṭha separates single words. And the Krama-pâṭha is two-fold, viz., the Varṇa-krama and the Pada-krama. The Varṇa-krama always doubles the first consonant of a group of consonants;

and the Pada-krama takes two words of the sentence together, and always reiterates the second of them with a following one. Of all the Prâtisâkhyas of the numerous Vaidik Samhitâs, the Prâtisâkhya belonging to the Sâkala-sâkhâ is by far the most complete.

There is another class of Sûtra works called the Anukramanîs. The Anukramanî to the Rig-veda is perfect in every respect. It is called the Sarvânukramanî which gives the first word of each hymn, the number of the verses, the names and families of the authors, the names of the deities to whom hymns are addressed, and the metre of every verse. Before the Sarvânukramanî was composed there existed separate indexes for each of the subjects, which were ascribed to Saunaka. The Sarvânukramanî is said to have been composed by Kâtyâyana. The Brihaddevatâ of Saunaka being very voluminous, is not reckoned among the Anukramanîs. It is composed in epic metre and contains an enumeration of the gods invoked in the hymns of the Rig-veda; and further supplies much valuable mythological information about the character of the deities of the Vedas. It is not unreasonable to suppose, judging from the general tenor and style of the Brihaddevatâ, that it was recast by a later writer. The Brihaddevatâ belongs to a much later period than most of the Sûtras; and it is, in fact, based upon the work of Yâska.* Dr. Kuhn infers from a passage in Shadgurusishya's commentary that not Saunaka but A'svalâyana was the author of the Brihaddevatâ. This inference, however, is not supported by suffi-

* Weber's Indische Studien, i. pp. 101-120; and his History of Indian Literature, p. 25.

cient evidence. *S*aunaka writes in mixed *s*lokas and breaks in many cases the laws of metre. Kâtyâyana writes in prose much after the fashion of the later Sûtras. The relation between *S*aunaka and Kâtyâyana was very intimate; and both of them belonged to the same *S*âkhâ. But it is probable that *S*aunaka was anterior to Kâtyâyana. The time of Sha*d*guru*s*ishya is not known. Probably his work was composed towards the close of the twelfth century.* There are three Anukrama*n*îs for the Yajur-veda, two for the Sâma-veda, and one for the Atharva-veda.†

The *R*ig-veda hymns are arranged according to two methods; the one having regard to the material bulk, and the other according to the authorship of the hymns. According to the former the whole Sa*m*hitâ consists of 8 *ashtakas* or eighths; these again are divided into 64 *adhyâyas* or lectures; these into 2006 *vargas* or sections; and the *vargas* into *richas* or verses, the actual number of which is 10,417; and some say that they amounted to 10,616 or 10,622. According to the other method, the Sa*m*hitâ is divided into 10 *mandalas* or circles; the *mandalas* into 85 *anuvâkas* or lessons, these into 1017 sûktas or hymns, besides eleven spurious ones, called Vâlakhilyas, and these again containing 10,580 and a half *richas*. The number of *padas* or words in this Sa*m*hitâ is stated as being 153,826, and that of the syllables is 432,000. The Nirukta mentions the *R*ig-veda in several places and always with the designation of Da*s*atayya or the ten parts. And the same mode of designation is also found in the

* Weber's Indische Studien, viii. p. 160, n.

† Müller's History of Ancient Sanskrit Literature, p. 215 ff.

Prâtisâkhya-Sûtras. Another instance of the systematic arrangement of the *mandalas* is contained in the A'pri-hymns; and there are only ten A'pri-Sûktas attached to the *R*ig-veda. These Sûktas consist properly of eleven verses, each of which is addressed to a separate deity; and they were evidently composed for sacrificial purposes. They, however, throw light on the social condition of the Indo-Aryans. The chief object of the A'pri hymns is not easy to explain. It is probable that the A'pri hymns were songs of reconciliation. *S*aunaka has given different names of metres in an Anukramanî. There are three Anukrama*n*is to the Yajus. The Sâman has two different Anukrama*n*îs. For the Atharvan, there is only one Anukrama*n*î which is called the B*r*ihatsarvânu-kramanî. The style of composition and the object of the different Anukrama*n*îs distinctly prove that they were framed at the close of the Vaidik age.*

There is a class of works commonly designated Parisish-*tas*. They have Vaidik rituals and sacrifices for their subject-matter. It is said that most of the Pari*s*ish*tas* are the productions of *S*aunaka, &c. The Parisish*tas* represent a distinct period of Indian literature, and they are evidently later than the Sûtras. Such literary works as the Pari*s*ish*tas* must be considered as the last outskirts of Vaidik literature. But still they are Vaidik in character. The Pari*s*ish*tas*, on the whole, are indited in simple and felicitous diction. They were originally eighteen in number, but that number has now considerably exceeded. The Chara*n*avyûha, though itself a Pari*s*ish*ta*, supports

* Müller's History of Ancient Sanskrit Literature, p. 215 ff.

this statement. There are a number of Parisishtas for each of the Vedas. For the Rig-veda there are only three, for the Sâma-veda the number is only six; and according to the Charanavyûha there exist eighteen Parisishtas for the Yajur-veda. But Prof. Weber fixes their number at seventy-four. The object of the Parisishtas is to supply the deficiencies in the Sûtras. They treat every thing in a popular and superficial manner. None of them were written probably before the middle of the third century, B. C. Though the Parisishtas are not held in the same estimation as other Vaidik works, yet they contain very interesting indications of the progress and decay of Hindû thought.

In former times the Vedas were the only source of knowledge and truth to the Hindûs. No one then ventured to carry on any controversy, or hold or spread any doctrine unwarranted by them, it being universally assumed that all doctrines must be based on, and all controversies must end in, what was taught by the Vedas. It was considered the height of atheism to speak one word against them. Thus it was that the supreme and unerring authority of the Vedas having been established, all theological controversy was at once nipped in the bud. On the othar hand, the study of the Vedas became gradually extinct; the understanding and explaining of their meanings became a hard task; the aims and objects of the *yajnas*, enjoined in them, were lost; and all religious works came to be encrusted with external ceremonies. In every country where religion becomes so dead and lifeless, religious changes begin to creep in. So did it fare with the Indian society. First of all *S*âkya, the founder of Buddhism, a man of uncommon wisdom and courage, opposed the Vedas, exposed the futility and unreasonableness of such of their doctrines as the killing of animals, and proved them to be of human origin. Men were surprised at the first starting of these novel theories of *S*âkya. They had long ago relinquished the use of reason under the despotic government of the Vedas ; but now again they entered the field of religious investigation, laid open by *S*âkya with renewed earnestness. But *S*âkya was not the first who opposed the selfish priesthood. Several centuries before him, Visvâmitra of the royal caste refused to submit to the hierarchical pretensions of the Brahmans, and succeeded in obtaining the privileges for which he determinately fought. King Janaka of Videha followed him in the same track. The spread of Buddhism was simply owing to the fact that it aimed at social reforms, and more so to its pure and simple morality rather than to the strength of its doctrinal points.

The doctrines of such a man as *S*âkya naturally began to spread with the rapidity of fire borne by driving winds, and India became a spacious field for the waging of religious wars. Thus, within a short period, the Buddhists waxed very strong in this country ; in the reign of Asoka, king of Magadha, the greater portion of it was converted to the religion of *S*âkya. The Brahmans again roused themselves and determined upon putting down the victorious heretics. With this view they went into every part of the country, stirred up the dormant spirit of the Hindû kings, and fell to religious debates with the Buddhists. In this momentous religious warfare *S*ankara A'châryа, who flourished in the 8th or 9th century,* played a most conspicuous and glorious part. He as a hermit visited alone every part of India, defeated the Buddhists, one and all, with the sharpedged acuteness of his intellect, his extraordinary wisdom and knowledge of the Vedas, and finally carried the palm of universal conquest. Thus, being borne down in debate by the Brahmans, and persecuted by kings, the Buddhists left India to spread their religion in other countries.† But though the Buddhists were themselves expelled from the country, their doctrines did not all follow them out of it; on the contrary, these doctrines began, day by day, to strike deep root. And the doctrines of *S*âkya were a refuge even for Brahmans, who were unable to master the extreme difficulties of their own complicated system.‡ The transcendental doctrine of Nirvâ*n*a, or total annihilation, which *S*âkya had proclaimed, was carefully picked up and and nursed by the Hindû philosophers. Buddhism if examined by its own canonical works, cannot be freed from the charge of Nihilism. *S*âkya himself not a Nihilist, was apparently an atheist. He does not gainsay either the existence of gods or that of God; but he denounces the former, and seems to be ignorant of the latter. If Nirvâ*n*a was not complete annihilation, it at any rate according to him, was absorption in the Divine essence. It was a relapse

* Colebrooke's Essays, i. p. 332.

† Troyer's Râdjatarangini, ii. p. 399.

‡ Burnouf's History of Indian Buddhism, p. 196.

into that Being which is nothing but itself. The original meaning of Nirvâna we can best know from the etymology of this technical term. Even a tyro in Sanskrit knows that Nirvâna means 'blowing out' and not absorption. The human soul when it reaches the acme of its full perfection, is blown out,* to use the phraseology of the Buddhists, like a lamp; it is not however absorbed, as the Brahmans say, like a drop in the ocean. We can not at all events accept the term Nirvâna in the sense of an apotheosis of the human soul as it is taught in the Vedânta philosophy. It admits of question whether the term Nirvâna was coined by Sâkya. Not merely different schools, but one and the same among the Buddhists appears to propound different theories as to the orthodox lexicography of this term.

The religion of the Vedas is an absurd system; Buddhism is equally absurd, but more philosophic. Buddhism was a revolt against the oppressive domination of the Brahmanic hierarchy. The devotion of the Buddhist ascetic was more disinterested. The Brahman idea of perfection was of an egotistical character. The meek spirit of Buddhism contrasts strongly with the haughtiness and arrogance of Brahmanism. We do not mean, however, to write the history of Buddhism; and we must, therefore, be satisfied with having given above a short sketch of a great revolution which occurred even in the Vaidik period.

There is one more circumstance in connexion with the subject to which we wish to allude, before we close,

* Amara-kosha, s. v.

and it has reference to the introduction of writing in ancient India. The greater portion of the vast ancient literature of India existed in oral tradition only, and was never reduced to writing. No man of any intelligence can easily imagine a civilized people unacquainted with the art of writing. If we are to understand that Hindû civilization could exist without a knowledge of writing, then it is needless to make reference to the arts, sciences, coins and measures, mentioned by Pâṇini in his Sûtras. From a certain rule of his (iv. 1, 49) we are convinced of the fact that he knew that writing was practised in countries beyond India. In that rule he teaches the formation of the word *Yavanânî*. Kâtyâyana and Patanjali define *Yavanânî* as meaning 'the writing of the *Yavanas*.' The word *Yavana* occurs in Homer as *Iaones* which is no doubt connected with the Hebrew *Yaṿan*. There can be no doubt that the Macedonian or Bactrian Greeks were the people most usually intended by the term. In later times it denoted especially the Arabs ; but in earlier times it was exclusively applied to the Greeks as is evident from a passage quoted in the commentary of Pâṇini's grammar, 'yavanâḥ ṣayânâ bhunjate,' which alludes, no doubt, to Greek customs. Weber* and not Müller† appears to give the meaning of the word *Yavanânî* as the writing of the Greeks alone ; but the latter would have us understand by it only a variety of the Semitic alphabet. M. Reinaud has given cogent reasons that *Yavanânî* means the writing of the Greeks. Benfey also understands by it 'Greek

* Indische Studien, i. p. 144 ; *Ibid*, iv. p. 89.

† History of Ancient Sanskrit Literature, p. 521.

writing.' *Yavanânî* was generally used to signify *lipi* or writing; and probably refers to the alphabet of the Greeks.

Müller says that in the grammar of Pânini there is not a single word which shows that the Hindûs knew the art of writing even when that learned work was composed. This assertion is a most novel and startling one, in as much as it is hard to conceive that a grammar, like that of Pânini, could be elaborated as it is now, without the advantage of written letters and signs in the days of the author. Kâtyâyana and Patanjali not merely presuppose a knowledge of writing in Pânini, but also affirm that the use he made of writing was one of the chief means which enabled him in building up the technical structure of his work. Any person that has ever looked into Pânini must know that written accents were indispensable for his terminology. Pânini uses accents as written signs. The *svarita* is the mark of an adhikâra or heading rule,* which showed a perpendicular line over the syllable; and the *anudâtta* a horizontal line under it. But the syllable which is without any such marks is *udâtta.* Pânini not unfrequently refers in his Sûtras to the grammarians who had preceded him; which circumstance strengthens the argument in favor of the fact that writing was known even before Pânini's time. Pânini teaches the formation of the word *lipikara* (iii. 2, 21); which can be adduced in all fairness, to prove that the greatest Grammarian of India was acquainted with the art of writing. The use of the term Patala, meaning a

* Pânini, i. 3, 11 : स्वरितेनाधिकारः ।

division of Sanskrit works, is a further proof that writing was known in ancient India.

The authors of the Sûtra works are found to apply the term *patala* to the short chapters of their works. It is, however, wholly absurd to suppose that chapters can be so called in a traditional work. It is only possible in a written one. Patala is almost synonymous with *liber* and *biblos*. "There is no word, says Müller, 'for book, paper, ink, writing, &c., in any Sanskrit work of genuine antiquity.'"* This assertion of Müller clearly shows that he has overlooked some words which might have, on the contrary, removed all his doubts. He should have known that the object of the Vaidik hymns is not to tell us that the Indo-Aryans had reed and ink. It is most difficult to suppose that the human mind could ever be capable of composing in prose, volume after volume, on rituals, long series of commentaries, and elaborate works on theology, grammar, and lexicography without the help of written letters. According to Wolf, prose composition is an evident and safe proof of a written literature as poetry without being committed to paper, could be easily composed and transmitted from one generation to another traditionally; but to compose any thing in prose is impossible without the help of writing; and still more impossible to transmit it from one generation to another and preserve it in its entirety traditionally.† There are undoubtedly records of astronomical observations which could not have been taken without the knowledge of numerical figures. We cannot

* History of Ancient Sanskrit Literature, p. 512.

† Wolf's Prolegomena, lxx-lxxiii.

help believing by the exact definition of words, which appear in Pâ*n*ini, such as var*n*a, kâra, kâ*nd*a, pattra, sûtra, adhyâya, grantha, &c., that the use of written letters was not unknown in ancient India. The meaning of the word *grantha* is to string together, signifying the old method of stringing together a number of palm leaves, which constituted the chief material of books, just as in German a volume is called *Band* from its being 'bound'. Prof. Weber holds that Pâ*n*ini was perfectly acquainted with the art of writing; and the word *grantha*, which is frequently used by Pâ*n*ini, alludes, according to its etymology, indisputably to written texts.* It answers etymologically to the Latin *textus*, as opposed to a traditional work. But Böhtlingk and Roth say, on the contrary, that the word *grantha* refers merely to the composition. Indeed, it may mean a literary composition. *Varna* applies only to a written sign; and *kára* to an uttered sound, and also to a written sign. *Akshara* means syllable; and may sometimes therefore coincide in value with *kâra* and *varna*. *Akshara* signifying 'syllable' first occurs in the Sa*m*hitâ of the Yajus. The word is also twice met with in the *R*ik; and there it signifies the measuring of speech (i. 164, 24 (47), and ix. 13, 3), and therefore may be used in the sense of 'syllable.' The Commentaries of Kâtyâyana, Patanjali and Kaiyya*t*a prove that Pâ*n*ini's manner of defining an *adhikâra* (i. 3, 11), or heading rule, would have been impossible without writing. Here we will draw the attention of the reader to two words, ûrdhva and ûdaya. The former is used adverbially in the

* Indische Studien, iv. p. 89.

sense of *after.** It seems to us that the metaphorical sense of the word was first applied to passages in written books. The word *ûdaya* is synonymous with *ûrdhva*. Pâ*n*ini speaks of *repha*. Even Kâtyâyana arguing from its root, concludes that it is nothing else than *ra* itself; and the letter *repha* is found to be used in the Prâtisâkhyas. The use of *repha* is also a proof that Pâ*n*ini was not ignorant of writing. *Grantha* occurs four times in the text of Pâ*n*ini; and it is evident, beyond doubt, that *grantha* must mean a written or bound book. In ancient times barks and leaves of particular trees were used as writing materials for want of paper. The Bhûrja-pattra and palm leaves were especially preferred. And even to this day Bhûrja-pattra and palm leaves are used for writing purposes. In Egypt this practice was also prevalent; and the very word paper is derived from 'papyrus' which means the bark of a reed.

The *S*rauta-Sûtras of A'*s*valâyana and the Prâtisâkhyas of the different Vedas contain numerous statements which cannot be explained without admitting a knowledge of letters on the part of the authors of those ancient works. Admitting that there is no allusion in the Vaidik hymns to writing, reading, paper, pen or anything else connected with writing this can never be a conclusive proof of the ignorance of the art of writing in ancient India. How were the gigantic works of ancient times divided into chapters and sections without any help of writing? How without a knowledge of numerals were the cattle marked on their ears in order to identify them?

* Manu, ix. 77.

Pâ*n*ini has a *sûtra* (vi. 3, 115) in which he says that the owners of cattle were at his time in the habit of marking their beasts on the ears, with signs of a svastika or magic figure of prosperity, a ladle, a pearl, &c., and also eight and five, which certainly point to a knowledge of written letters or numerals at that period. Similarly the use of *lopa*, to express elision,* as opposed to the visibility of a letter points to language as existing in a written and not exclusively spoken form. It is impossible that an author could speak of a thing visible, literally or metaphorically, unless it were referable to his sense of sight. A letter which has undergone the effect of *lopa*, must, therefore, previously to its *lopa*, have been a visible or written letter to him. Every one must now understand that Pâ*n*ini was as proficient in writing as the cowherds of his time. It will not also be rash to hold that the Vedas were preserved in writing at or before Pâ*n*ini's time. And it could be easily shown that Pâ*n*ini must have seen written Vaidik texts.† Now, it is obvious thât the ancient Hindûs must have been acquainted with the art of writing. No question can be raised against the fact that the Hindûs were acquainted with the art of writing before the time of Alexander ; and the expressions *likhita* and *likhâpita*‡ occur in the inscriptions of Piyadasi, which are, no doubt, of the third century B. C. However, we shall not exceed a reasonable limit by assigning the 13th century B. C. to the origin of writing in India.

* Pâ*n*ini, i. 1, 60 : अदर्शनं लोपः ।

† Pâ*n*ini, vii. 1, 76 : छन्दस्यपि दृश्यते ।

‡ Manu, viii. 168.

What was the alphabet that Pāṇini and his predecessors used, is a question that can hardly be answered positively since there are not sufficient data to decide it. But it was by no means the Bactrian. The Bactrian is avowedly not full. Its vowels are few and at the same time not perfect, and even its consonants are deficient. In such a case the Bactrian could have been, by no means, originally adopted and used for a language most noted for its long and short vowels. To suppose that when a nation had once caught the idea of alphabetic writing, they would afterwards fail to devise a sufficient number of letters to meet their requirements, is quite absurd. It is also said that they must have got their alphabet from the Dravidians who were autochthonous in India; and from no other source. But there is nothing to prove that these aborigines had a written literature at the time when the Aryans intruded on them and settled here. Not even now has a single Dravidian book been discovered, which may be considered to be of a pre-Vaidik era. The Dravidians were by no means a literary race, their ancient history is quite a blank; and the little that we know of them is from the writings of the Indo-Aryans themselves. That when the Dravidians themselves had no alphabet of their own, the Indo-Aryans borrowed one from them, is so illogical that it scarcely calls for further notice. It is supposed by some that the Aryans did not originate an alphabet either before they migrated to India or after they settled here; but they must have borrowed elsewhere. According to them the writing of the Indo-Aryans is of Semitic origin.* Assuming that they came to India before they had devised a system of alphabetic writing, it will not be paradoxcial to hazard an opinion (more especially when they are said to have left their primitive home in a far more advanced social state than their predecessors who had long before separated from them, and gone forth in other directions,) that such a highly intellectual race as the Indo-Aryans would originate it in their adopted country, without borrowing it from their neighbours.

* Benfey, Indien (in Ersch and Gruber's Encyclopædia, 1840), p. 254; Weber's Indische Skizzen (1856), p. 127 ff; and Burnell's Elements of South Indian Palæography, p. 3 ff.

APPENDIX.

The PURUSHA-SUKTA, or the 90th Hymn of the 10th Book of the Rig-veda Samhitâ.

1. Purusha has a thousand heads, a thousand eyes, a thousand feet. On every side enveloping the earth, he overpassed (it) by a space of ten fingers. 2. Purusha himself is this whole (universe), whatever has been and whatever shall be. He is also the lord of immortality, since (or, when) by food he expands. 3. Such is his greatness, and Purusha is superior to this. All existences are a quarter of him; and three-fourths of him are that which is immortal in the sky. 4. With three quarters Purusha mounted upwards. A quarter of him was again produced here. He was then diffused everywhere over things which eat and things which do not eat. 5. From him was born Virâj, and from Virâj, Purusha. When born, he extended beyond the earth, both behind and before. 6. When the gods performed a sacrifice with Purusha as the oblation, the spring was its butter, the summer its fuel, and the autumn its (accompanying) offering. 7. This victim, Purusha, born in the beginning, they immolated on the

sacrificial grass. With him the gods, the Sâdhyas, and the *r*ishis sacrificed. 8. From that universal sacrifice were provided curds and butter. It formed those aerial (creatures) and animals both wild and tame. 9. From that universal sacrifice sprang the *r*ich-, sâman-, and chhandas-, verses: from it sprang the yajus. 10. From it sprang horses, and all animals with two rows of teeth; kine sprang irom it; from it goats and sheep. 11. When (the gods) divided Purusha, into how many parts did they cut him up? what was his mouth? what arms (had he)? what (two objects) are said (to have been) his thighs and feet? 12. The Brahman was his mouth; the Râjanya was made his arms; the being (called) the Vai*s*ya, he was his thighs; the *S*ûdra sprang from his feet. 13. The moon sprang from his soul (*manas*), the sun from his eye, Indra and Agni from his mouth, and Vâyu from his breath. 14. From his navel arose the air, from his head the sky, from his feet the earth, from his ear the (four) quarters: in this manner (the gods) formed the worlds. 15. When the gods, performing sacrifice, bound Purusha as a victim, there were seven sticks (stuck up) for it (around the fire), and thrice seven pieces of fuel were made. 16. With sacrifice the gods performed the sacrifice. These were the earliest rites. These great powers have sought the sky, where are the former Sâdhyas, gods.

JOHN MUIR.

PRINTED AT THE BARAT PRESS, CALCUTTA.